Baking Magic WITH Aquafaba

Transform Your Favorite Vegan Treats with the Revolutionary New Egg Substitute

Kelsey Kinser

Ulysses Press

Published in the United States by
ULYSSES PRESS
P.O. Box 3440
Berkeley, CA 94703
www.ulyssespress.com

ISBN: 978-1-61243-721-7
Library of Congress Control Number: 2017937992

Printed in the United States by United Graphics Inc.
10 9 8 7 6 5 4 3 2 1

Acquisitions editor: Casie Vogel
Managing editor: Claire Chun
Project editor: Alice Riegert
Editor: Renee Rutledge
Proofreader: Shayna Keyles
Front cover design: Michelle Thompson
Cover photographs: macarons © Evgeny Karandaev/shutterstock.com; shortcake © Yuliia Mazurkevych/shutterstock.com; meringue © Nadia Brusnikova/shutterstock.com; chocolate cake © Africa Studio/shutterstock.com

Distributed by Publishers Group West

NOTE: This book is independently authored and published and no sponsorship or endorsement of this book by, and no affiliation with, any trademarked brands or other products mentioned within is claimed or suggested. All trademarks that appear in ingredient lists and elsewhere in this book belong to their respective owners and are used here for informational purposes only. The author and publisher encourage readers to patronize the quality brands mentioned and pictured in this book.

This book is dedicated to my loving husband, Shany David.
Thanks for putting up with the obscene amount of time I spend in the kitchen. I love you.

CONTENTS

INTRODUCTION

Aquafaba, also known as bean water, is a magic liquid that has given vegan baking a serious lift. That's because it acts like egg whites in many ways. It can be used as an egg substitute in all of your favorite baked good recipes. It makes cheese that melts and meringues that fluff up and stay that way. Did I mention it also lightens frostings? Or works in place of an egg wash on breads? Yes, it does all this and more!

So, what is this magic liquid? Aquafaba comes from soaking certain legumes. For the purposes of this book, this always means the liquid from a can of chickpeas or from cooking your own chickpeas, unless other beans are specifically called for. Chickpeas tend to give the most stable and neutral-flavored aquafaba, which makes it suitable for any recipe. The reason for this is currently unknown, but people are continuing to experiment with the soaking liquid of other beans.

Aquafaba may work a lot like a raw egg white, but it has a very different composition. Egg whites are primarily protein with water; aquafaba is primarily water, with starch and some protein. This means that, sadly, aquafaba (AF) is not strong enough to support a recipe like a classic angel food cake. Don't be discouraged, however. The world is full of amazingly talented vegan bakers who work tirelessly to come up with the next evolution in the world of cruelty-free pastries. In fact, aquafaba has only been used in this manner since the end of 2014, when French chef Joël Roessel discovered it. New food miracles are happening all the time, and this book should have enough to keep you busy for a while.

In this book, you will learn how to use aquafaba to advance your baking with recipes for soft, spongy cakes, rich and creamy ice creams, cheese substitutes that melt, and more. You'll learn how to set yourself up for AF success, how to troubleshoot failures, and how to branch out and create your own flavor variations once you've mastered the basics. With the knowledge provided in this book and some practice, you will be on a path to unlimited vegan baking possibilities.

This book starts out with recipes for making and storing your own aquafaba so that you can bake at a moment's notice, while also informing you how to use aquafaba from store-bought canned chickpeas. After you've got your bean water ready, you will start with a plethora of breakfast recipes, then move on to cakes and frostings, candies, mousses and pies, cookies, macarons, ice creams, holiday specials, savory treats, and lastly, spreads and dips. (And, yes, macarons are cookies, but they're so special that I gave them their own chapter.)

I like to work from base recipes, meaning I will start with a basic formula for something like ice cream and then I will alter that base recipe to make variations. This is part of my background working in professional kitchens. You'll see what I mean with recipes like the buttercreams, macarons, and ice creams. Once you become comfortable with the base recipes, you can be creative with your ingredients.

You will find a recipe for homemade aquafaba butter in this book. You can substitute this homemade item for any recipe calling for vegan butter. Alternatively, if you do not want to make your own butter, any good store-bought brand can work. Also note that I do not count cooking spray as an ingredient, and each recipe will tell you if you need to spray the pan or not. Sometimes you want your pans sprayed to allow a quick release of your baked good, and sometimes you deliberately want your confection to stick to the pan so that it rises while baking or holds the correct shape. I like to use a neutral-flavored spray like coconut or canola oil.

Note: Remember the aquafaba is always thinner when it is hot! Use only cool or room-temperature AF. Excess aquafaba can be frozen in ice cube trays for future use.

Before You Get Started

Baking and candy making can move very fast once things get started, which is why you always want your *mise en place*. This is a fancy French way of saying to make sure you have all of your ingredients measured out, and all of your equipment ready. This way you can complete a recipe with no hiccups in the middle that could lead to disastrous results.

In many recipes for meringues or whipped AF that I find on the Internet, recipe writers will call for the beaters to be set on high. I'm not a fan of this as the rapid whipping creates uneven bubbles in the meringue mixture. Why are uneven bubbles an issue? Imagine your meringue is full of 40 percent small bubbles and 60 percent large bubbles. If your large bubbles pop, you'll experience a much greater deflation than if your meringue were made up of 80 percent small bubbles. Five popped small bubbles is less noticeable than five popped large bubbles. This is why I always start on medium speed.

Troubleshooting

Aquafaba takes some getting used to, and to be completely honest, sometimes it works, sometimes it doesn't, but there are steps to help ensure you're starting on the best possible foot. The first thing to remember is not all aquafabas are created equal. If you are using AF from a can, you will find some brands work better than others, and it may just take time and experimentation to find what works for you. I have found some of the smaller, organic brands like Brad's Organic work very well. No matter what, you want salt-free or reduced salt aquafaba.

In this book, you will find two recipes to make your own AF, one using a stove and another using a slow cooker. Always make sure, whether you get it from a can or make it, that you strain your AF! Stray pieces of chickpea can devastate the bubbles in a fluffy meringue and bring down an otherwise light and airy cake. Straining prevents stray items from getting into your baked good.

....

A Note on Oven Temperatures

It's said that every time you open the oven, you lose 25°F. A longer preheat period allows the walls of your oven to truly heat through, which means that your temperature will bounce back a lot quicker. How do you know you have the correct level of heat kicking in your hot box? Well, certainly, you have an oven thermometer, don't you? You don't? For around $5 a pop, why the heck not? No single gadget will save you more time, money, and heartache when it comes to pastry endeavors of all types.

I always use light-colored baking trays. If yours are dark (most nonstick ones are) lower your oven temperature by 25°F.

Lastly, learn to trust yourself. If you are sure that four hours is enough time to cool something, then go for it. Once you are comfortable with the processes and know the hows and whys behind the science of baking, you'll be unstoppable.

....

Some recipes call for reduced aquafaba. This is AF that has been simmered down by anywhere from ⅓ to ½ cup. Other recipes don't require it. I have found that making my own aquafaba and then reducing it gives me the strongest, most reliable AF possible. Regardless of the recipe, I like to use reduced, cold aquafaba, which most realistically mimics egg whites. Try to use unreduced AF in a recipe that needs something strong and you'll most likely have a flop. Use reduced AF in a recipe that doesn't need it and you'll suffer no ills at all. This is why I just like to go ahead and make a bulk batch, reduce it, and then freeze it in 1 tablespoon ice cube trays for quick use.

The Internet is a great resource if you seem to be struggling despite following all of the steps. This wonderful bean water is a very recent discovery and new uses are continuously being discovered. There is a wildly popular Facebook Group called "Vegan Meringues: Hits and Misses!" where you can post a question on a recipe you have and receive feedback, sometimes instantly.

✳ Slow Cooker Aquafaba

Using a slow cooker is the easiest way to make your own AF. Presoak the beans for at least an hour if you want to prevent them from splitting while they cook (optional, but recommended if you intend to use the beans whole in other recipes). While the overnight refrigeration cool is not necessary, I find it helps out greatly. You can halve this recipe, but I find a halved recipe works better on the stovetop than in the slow cooker.

12 cups water

pinch kosher salt

4 cups (2 pounds) dried chickpeas, rinsed well

1. If you have the time, soak the chickpeas in warm (not hot) water for at least an hour.

2. Place the water and salt together in a pot with a lid. Cover and bring to a boil.

3. Place the chickpeas into your slow cooker. Carefully pour the boiling water over the chickpeas. Cook on low for 8 to 10 hours.

4. Remove the slow cooker insert and allow the beans and liquid to cool together in the slow cooker insert until it reaches room temperature. Drain the aquafaba from the chickpeas and store both in the fridge. (You can use the chickpeas immediately if so desired.) Allow the aquafaba to rest in the refrigerator overnight.

Note: Remember the aquafaba is always thinner when it is hot! Use only cool or room-temperature AF. Excess aquafaba can be frozen in ice cube trays for future use.

YIELD: 6 cups aquafaba, plus 14 cups cooked chickpeas   PREP TIME: 10 minutes, plus at least one hour to soak (optional)   COOK TIME: 8 to 10 hours, plus overnight cooling

❋ Stovetop Aquafaba

Homemade aquafaba is as easy as can be, and it's significantly cheaper than using canned juice. It does, however, require at least one night (or a very full day) to soak the dried chickpeas, which is entirely inactive time but still must be accounted for. This recipe can easily be doubled.

2 cups (1 pound) dried chickpeas, rinsed well

5 cups water

pinch kosher salt

1. Place the rinsed chickpeas into a large container fitted with a lid. Cover the chickpeas with the water and seal the container. Allow the chickpeas to soak for 12 hours. Save the soaking water!

2. Move the chickpeas and soaking water into a small pot. Add the salt and more water if there is not enough to cover the beans. Turn the heat up to medium high and bring the contents of the pot to a boil. Reduce the heat until the peas and water are at a simmer, and allow to cook until the chickpeas are tender, anywhere between 45 minutes to an hour, depending on your chickpeas. If at any point during this process the water level gets too low and does not cover the beans, add just enough water until they are covered.

3. Drain the cooking liquid into a heat-proof vessel, like a jar. Allow the mixture to cool in the fridge. At this point it should be thicker and nice and viscous, exactly as it looks when it comes out of a can. If it is still water-thin, place the aquafaba back into a small pot and simmer to reduce by 10 to 20 percent more, or until the liquid has thickened. It will thicken up as it cools.

Note: Remember the aquafaba is always thinner when it is hot! Use only cool or room-temperature AF. Excess aquafaba can be frozen in ice cube trays for future use.

YIELD: approximately 3 cups aquafaba, plus 7 cups cooked chickpeas   PREP TIME: 10 minutes, plus 12 hour soak time   COOK TIME: 1 hour, plus overnight cooling

BREAKFAST

Breakfast is the meal of the day with the most options going for it. Do you want to start your day with something sweet? Something salty? Light? Heavy? It's the most important meal of the day and no one will look at you twice if you make that meal cake—so long as those are *pan*cakes, that is. And let's not forget waffles and muffins, both essentially desserts. But before you get overloaded with thoughts of starting every day on a sugar high, contained in this chapter are also recipes for carrot lox, bacon, quiche, and many more savory breakfast goodies. Thank goodness for breakfast!

❋ Crunchy Granola Clusters

Granola has long been associated with health food, despite the fact that it is often full of oil and sugar, or both! This recipe uses aquafaba and bananas to cut down on the oil and the sugar and create a naturally lighter option. Pressing down on the granola before baking helps it to stay clumped together in delectable clusters.

2 very ripe bananas	2 teaspoons ground cinnamon
2 tablespoons aquafaba	pinch ground cloves
¼ cup peanut butter	½ teaspoon kosher salt
¼ cup maple syrup	3 cups old-fashioned rolled oats (not instant)
2 tablespoons refined coconut oil, melted	1½ cups chopped walnuts

1. Preheat your oven to 350°F. Line a baking tray with either a silicone baking sheet or parchment paper. If using parchment, brush it lightly with coconut oil.

2. In a large bowl, mash the bananas with the aquafaba, peanut butter, and maple syrup. Once this is mixed, stir in the melted coconut oil.

3. Mix the remaining ingredients into the banana mixture, stirring until well combined.

4. Spread this mixture as evenly as possible onto the baking tray. Using a large, flat spatula, press down firmly on all of the unbaked granola. It should start to stick together.

5. Bake for 35 to 40 minutes, stirring every 10 minutes and rotating the tray if needed, until the granola has gotten all toasty brown. Cool before serving or storing.

YIELD: 5 cups   PREP TIME: 5 to 10 minutes   COOK TIME: 35 to 40 minutes

 # Waffles

Waffles, what more can I say about them? This is a classic French recipe that makes a much lighter waffle than anything you'd find in your grocer's freezer. Serve warm with Aquafaba and maple syrup and/or with fruit.

1 tablespoon white vinegar	pinch cream of tartar or 4 drops lemon juice
2½ cups almond milk	3 tablespoons sugar
3 cups all-purpose flour	1 teaspoon vanilla extract
⅛ teaspoon kosher salt	¼ cup coconut oil, melted
⅔ cup aquafaba	

1. In a small bowl, stir the vinegar into the almond milk and set aside for at least 5 minutes. This makes it much more like buttermilk.

2. In a separate bowl, mix the flour with the salt.

3. Using a stand mixer, combine your aquafaba and cream of tartar or lemon juice, and whip on medium speed for about 5 minutes. You want to beat the aquafaba to soft peaks, which means that when you remove the whisk, the tip of the peak will collapse/fold over.

4. With the mixer still on medium, slowly sprinkle in the sugar. Continue to beat until the meringues are thick, shiny, and stiff peaked. Mix in the vanilla and the melted coconut oil until fully combined.

5. Stir together the almond milk mixture with the flour mixture. Fold the meringue into the milk and flour batter until mixed together.

6. Preheat your waffle iron until it is hot and ready.

7. Once the pan is hot, spray with nonstick spray and ladle a ¼- to ½-cup scoop of batter, depending on the size of your waffle iron.

8. Cook according to your waffle iron instructions.

YIELD: 8 to 12 waffles, depending on size of waffle maker   PREP TIME: 20 minutes
COOK TIME: 15 minutes

❉ Chocolate "Malted" Waffle

This recipe is for when you want to start your day off sweet, but not cloyingly so. The maca root powder recreates that nutty toasted flavor of malted milk powder, while also giving you a bit of a super food boost. This is a breakfast that seems worse for you than it is. Serve warm with Aquafaba and maple syrup and/or fruit.

1 tablespoon white vinegar

2½ cups almond milk

2 cups all-purpose flour

½ cup maca root powder

½ cup cocoa powder

⅛ teaspoon kosher salt

⅔ cup aquafaba

pinch cream of tartar or 4 drops lemon juice

¼ cup sugar

½ teaspoon vanilla extract

¼ cup coconut oil, melted

1. In a small bowl, stir the vinegar into the almond milk and set aside for at least 5 minutes. This makes it much more like buttermilk.

2. In a separate bowl, mix the flour with the maca root powder, cocoa powder, and salt.

3. Using a stand mixer, combine your aquafaba and cream of tartar or lemon juice, and whip on medium speed for about 5 minutes. You want to beat the aquafaba to soft peaks, which means that when you remove the whisk, the tip of the peak will collapse/fold over.

4. With the mixer still on medium, slowly sprinkle in the sugar. Continue to beat until the meringues are thick, shiny, and stiff peaked. Mix in the vanilla and the melted coconut oil until fully combined.

5. Stir together the almond milk mixture with the flour mixture. Fold the meringue into the milk and flour batter until mixed together.

6. Preheat your waffle iron until it is hot and ready.

7. Once the pan is hot, ladle a ¼- to ½-cup scoop of batter, depending on the size of your waffle iron.

8. Cook according to your waffle iron instructions.

YIELD: 8 to 12 waffles, depending on size of waffle maker   PREP TIME: 20 minutes
COOK TIME: 15 minutes

✳ Birthday Cake Waffles

On my birthday every year, my parents would wake me up with the Beatles' song "Birthday" and a piece of cake. Now that I'm living on my own, I like to make these confetti pancakes for special occasions (not just birthdays) and any other day that needs some little pops of color. Using imitation vanilla extract gives you that nostalgic flavor, but you can use regular vanilla if you'd prefer. Serve warm with whipped coconut cream or meringue on top.

1½ cups all-purpose flour	⅓ cup aquafaba
1 cup sugar	1½ cups almond milk
1½ teaspoons baking powder	1 teaspoon imitation vanilla extract
½ teaspoon baking soda	⅓ cup Homemade Sprinkles (page 56)
¼ teaspoon kosher salt	

1. In a medium bowl, stir the flour with the sugar, baking powder, baking soda, and salt.

2. In another bowl, mix the aquafaba, oatmilk, and vanilla until combined.

3. Stir the liquid mix into the dry mix until just combined. Stir in the sprinkles.

4. Preheat your waffle iron until it is hot and ready.

5. Once the pan is hot, ladle a ¼- to ½-cup scoop of batter, depending on the size of your waffle iron.

6. Cook according to your waffle iron instructions.

YIELD: 8 to 12 waffles, depending on size of waffle maker   PREP TIME: 10 minutes
COOK TIME: 15 minutes

 # Pancakes

Aquafaba really elevates the breakfast table, which should come as no surprise as it's capable of tackling most of the jobs that, for so long, only eggs were able to do. These fluffy and flavorful blueberry pancakes come together quickly once everything is measured out. Feel free to substitute any other berry or chopped fruit in place of the blueberries. Raspberries with a teaspoon of lemon zest are one of my favorite variations, and fresh or dried cranberries with orange zest is a lovely fall-ready treat. If you absolutely have to have your pancakes perfect looking, leave the blueberries out of the batter until you pour the batter into the skillet. Then you can drop the berries into the pancakes in exactly the spots you want them to be, so every bite will be perfect.

⅓ cup aquafaba

pinch cream of tartar or 4 drops lemon juice

1 cup almond milk

2 teaspoons distilled white vinegar

¼ cup sugar

1 teaspoon vanilla extract

3 tablespoons vegetable oil, plus more for cooking

1½ cups all-purpose flour

½ teaspoon baking soda

½ teaspoon baking powder

½ cup blueberries

Aquafaba Butter (page 128) and maple syrup, to serve

1. Using a stand mixer, combine your aquafaba and cream of tartar or lemon juice, and whip on medium speed for about 5 minutes. You want to beat the aquafaba to soft peaks, which means that when you remove the whisk, the tip of the peak will collapse/fold over.

2. While the aquafaba whips up, combine the almond milk and vinegar in a separate bowl and set aside, allowing it to sour.

3. With the mixer still on medium, slowly sprinkle in the sugar. Continue to beat until the meringues are thick, shiny, and stiff peaked. Mix in the vanilla.

4. Whisk the vegetable oil into the soured milk. Set aside.

5. In a large bowl, mix together the flour, baking soda, and baking powder.

6. Pour the milk mixture into the flour mix and stir until almost combined. Gently stir in the blueberries.

7. Set your stove to medium heat and warm up a large pan or skillet. Let the pan get nice and hot while you gently fold the pancake batter into the aquafaba in three batches, taking care to deflate the mix as little as possible.

8. Once everything is just combined and the pan is hot, drop a spoonful of vegetable oil into the pan followed by even, ¼-cup scoops of batter.

9. Allow the pancakes to cook until their edges are set and bubbles start to pop through to the top, 2 to 3 minutes. Flip once and cook until golden brown on both sides.

10. Serve topped with Aquafaba Butter and syrup.

YIELD: 12 (5-inch) pancakes   PREP TIME: 10 minutes   COOK TIME: 15 minutes

❋ Double-Chocolate Pancakes

This is the breakfast for choc-o-holics: cocoa pancakes studded with chocolate chips and topped with chocolate sauce. Pain au Chocolat has nothing on this level of chocolate. If you like your chocolate sweet, then use (vegan) milk chocolate chips and sauce. If you use dark chocolate, these pancakes will be richer and deeper than with the milk chocolate variety. If you're making these pancakes for children, you may want to do a mixture of the sweeter milk chocolate chips with a darker fudge sauce.

⅓ cup aquafaba

pinch cream of tartar or drop of lemon juice

1 cup almond milk

2 teaspoons distilled white vinegar

¼ cup sugar

1 teaspoon vanilla extract

2 tablespoons vegetable oil, plus more for cooking

1¼ cups all-purpose flour

¼ cup cocoa powder

½ teaspoon baking soda

½ teaspoon baking powder

⅓ cup chocolate chips

vegan chocolate sauce, to serve

1. Using a stand mixer, combine your aquafaba and cream of tartar or lemon juice, and whip on medium speed for about 5 minutes. You want to beat the aquafaba to soft peaks, which means that when you remove the whisk, the tip of the peak will collapse/fold over.

2. While the aquafaba whips up, combine the almond milk and vinegar in a separate bowl and set aside, allowing it to sour for at least 5 minutes.

3. With the mixer still on medium, slowly sprinkle in the sugar. Continue to beat until the meringues are thick, shiny, and stiff peaked. Mix in the vanilla.

4. Whisk the vegetable oil into the soured milk. Set aside.

5. In a large bowl, mix together the flour, cocoa powder, baking soda, and baking powder.

6. Pour the milk mixture into the flour mix and stir until almost combined. Gently stir in the chocolate chips.

7. Set your stove to medium heat and warm up a large pan or skillet. Let the pan get nice and hot while you gently fold the pancake batter into the aquafaba in three batches, taking care to deflate the mix as little as possible.

8. Once everything is just combined and the pan is hot, drop a spoonful of vegetable oil into the pan, followed by even, ¼-cup scoops of batter.

9. Allow the pancakes to cook until their edges are set and bubbles start to pop through to the top, 2 to 3 minutes. Flip once and cook until golden brown on both sides.

10. Serve topped with vegan chocolate sauce.

YIELD: 12 (5-inch) pancakes   PREP TIME: 15 minutes   COOK TIME: 15 minutes

❀ Whole Wheat Pain D'Epice Pancakes

Pain D'Epice, or spice bread, is a French treat sweetened with honey. In this recipe, I use brown rice syrup, though agave or golden syrup could work as well. It's traditionally a rather dense cake. Using whole wheat pastry flour gives these pancakes a hearty bite, without sacrificing the light airiness one looks for in a pancake.

⅓ cup aquafaba

pinch cream of tartar or drop lemon juice, optional

1 cup almond milk

2 teaspoons distilled white vinegar

1 tablespoon sugar

1 teaspoon vanilla extract

2 tablespoons vegetable oil, plus more for cooking

2 tablespoons brown rice syrup or agave

½ teaspoon ground cinnamon

½ teaspoon ground ginger

pinch ground cloves

pinch fresh ground nutmeg

1½ cups whole wheat pastry flour

½ teaspoon baking soda

½ teaspoon baking powder

Aquafaba Butter (page 128) and maple syrup, to serve

1. Using a stand mixer, combine your aquafaba and cream of tartar or lemon juice, and whip on medium speed for about 5 minutes. You want to beat the aquafaba to soft peaks, which means that when you remove the whisk, the tip of the peak will collapse/fold over.

2. While the aquafaba whips up, combine the almond milk and vinegar in a separate bowl and set aside, allowing it to sour for at least 5 minutes.

3. With the mixer still on medium, slowly sprinkle in the sugar. Continue to beat until the meringues are thick, shiny, and stiff peaked. Mix in the vanilla.

4. Whisk the vegetable oil and brown rice syrup (or agave) into the soured milk. Set aside.

5. In a large bowl, mix together the spices, whole wheat flour, baking soda, and baking powder.

6. Pour the milk mixture into the flour mix, and stir until just combined.

7. Set your stove to medium heat and warm up a large pan or skillet. Let the pan get nice and hot while you gently fold the pancake batter into the aquafaba in three batches, taking care to deflate the mix as little as possible.

8. Once everything is just combined and the pan is hot, drop a spoonful of vegetable oil into the pan, followed by even-sized scoops of batter.

9. Allow the pancakes to cook until their edges are set and bubbles start to pop through to the top, 2 to 3 minutes. Flip once and cook until golden brown on both sides.

10. Serve topped with Aquafaba Butter and maple syrup.

YIELD: 12 (5-inch) pancakes   PREP TIME: 15 minutes   COOK TIME: 15 minutes

❄ Whole Wheat Cinnamon Scones

My favorite scone is a spiced, whole wheat one. The hearty bite of the wheat makes for a fully satisfying breakfast. I prefer to serve these scones warm. Serve leftovers lightly toasted in a toaster or regular oven, slathered with Aquafaba Butter or jam.

½ teaspoon vinegar

½ cup plus 2 tablespoons almond milk, divided

2 cups whole wheat flour

¼ cup sugar

¾ teaspoon kosher salt

1 tablespoon baking powder

½ teaspoon baking soda

½ teaspoon ground cinnamon, plus more for sprinkling

3 tablespoons aquafaba

1 teaspoon vanilla extract

½ cup cold Aquafaba Butter (page 128), cubed

1. In a small bowl, mix the vinegar into the ½ cup almond milk and set aside until the milk is slightly thickened and tangy, about 5 minutes.

2. Prepare a baking sheet by lining it with parchment paper.

3. In a large bowl, sift together the flour, sugar, salt, baking powder, baking soda, and cinnamon.

4. Stir the aquafaba and vanilla into the milk mixture. Set aside.

5. Cut the butter into the flour mixture using a pastry cutter/dough blender or a couple of forks, or by pulsing the mix in a food processor. Mix until the dough is full of pebbles of butter. These "pebbles" do not need to be the same size and some variation is preferred. This gives the scone its texture. You want this to be just undermixed.

6. Add the milk mixture to the flour mixture and stir using a firm spoon or spatula. Stir until just combined.

7. Lightly flour the prepared baking sheet. Divide the dough into two equal pieces. Shape these pieces on the baking sheet into circles, about 6 inches in diameter.

8. Brush the tops of the circles with remaining 2 tablespoons of milk.

9. Run a sharp knife under cold water and cut the circles into 6 pieces each. Separate the pieces from one another until there is a space of ½ inch between them.

10. Place the scones in the freezer for 30 minutes. While the scones chill, preheat the oven to 425°F.

11. Bake the scones for about 25 minutes or until they are golden brown. Remove from the oven and sprinkle with additional cinnamon.

12. Cool for 5 minutes and serve warm.

YIELD: 12 scones   PREP TIME: 10 minutes   COOK TIME: 25 minutes, plus 30 minutes of chilling

❈ Cranberry Orange Scones

While scones are a classic baked good from the British Isles, the flavoring of cranberries and orange is distinctly American.

½ teaspoon vinegar

½ cup plus 2 tablespoons almond milk, divided

2¾ cups all-purpose flour

⅓ cup sugar

¾ teaspoon kosher salt

1 tablespoon baking powder

¼ cup plus 2 tablespoons aquafaba

½ cup cold Aquafaba Butter (page 128), cubed

1½ cups dried cranberries

1 tablespoon orange zest

½ teaspoon ground cinnamon

1. In a small bowl, mix the vinegar into the ½ cup almond milk and set aside until milk is slightly thickened and tangy, about 5 minutes.

2. Prepare a baking sheet by lining it with parchment paper.

3. In a large bowl, sift together the flour, sugar, salt, and baking powder. Stir the aquafaba into the milk mixture. Set aside.

4. Cut the butter into the flour mixture using a pastry cutter/dough blender or a couple of forks, or by pulsing the mix in a food processor. Mix until the dough is full of pebbles of butter. These "pebbles" do not need to be the same size and some variation is preferred. This gives the scone its texture. You want this to be just undermixed.

5. Mix in the cranberries, orange zest, and cinnamon. Add the milk mixture to the flour mixture and stir using a firm spoon or spatula until just combined.

6. Lightly flour the prepared baking sheet. Divide the dough into two equal pieces. Shape these pieces on the baking sheet into circles, about 6 inches in diameter.

7. Brush the tops of the circles with the remaining 2 tablespoons of milk.

8. Run a sharp knife under cold water and cut the circles into 6 pieces each. Separate the pieces from one another until there is a space of ½ inch between them. Place the scones in the freezer for 30 minutes. While the scones chill, preheat the oven to 425°F.

9. Bake the scones for about 25 minutes or until they are golden brown. Cool for 5 minutes and serve warm.

YIELD: 12 scones   PREP TIME: 10 minutes   COOK TIME: 25 minutes, plus 30 minutes of chilling

❋ Lemon Poppy Seed Muffins

What a classic flavor combination. Save your money and a hearty dose of calories by making this cafe favorite at home.

2⅔ cups all-purpose flour

2 teaspoons baking powder

¼ teaspoon baking soda

1 teaspoon kosher salt

1 cup white sugar

¼ cup plus 2 tablespoons aquafaba

2 teaspoons lemon zest

¼ cup lemon juice

¼ cup almond milk

1½ teaspoons vanilla extract

¼ cup coconut oil, melted

3 tablespoons poppy seed

2 tablespoons raw sugar

1. Preheat the oven to 375°F. Prepare a muffin tin with liners.

2. In a large bowl, sift together the flour, baking powder, baking soda, salt, and sugar. Set aside.

3. In a separate bowl, stir together the aquafaba, lemon zest, lemon juice, almond milk, and vanilla.

4. Add the liquid to the flour mixture and stir until nearly combined. Add in the coconut oil and poppy seeds.

5. Scoop the muffin mixture into the prepared muffin tin and sprinkle with the raw sugar.

6. Bake for 30 to 35 minutes or until the muffins have puffed up and the tops are golden.

7. Allow to cool completely before serving.

YIELD: **12 muffins**   PREP TIME: **10 minutes**   COOK TIME: **30 to 35 minutes**

❋ Bran Muffins

Bran muffins are the most underrated muffin, and they are my personal favorite. Bran muffins should be hearty, moist, and finished with a touch of sweetness. They should never be so dry that you can't eat one without a cup of coffee, though they do go great with a cup of joe. Bran muffins should have you feeling full until lunchtime.

1 cup almond milk

1 teaspoon cider vinegar

1 cup whole wheat flour

2 teaspoons baking powder

½ teaspoon baking soda

½ teaspoon kosher salt

1½ cups wheat bran

⅓ cup mashed ripe banana

¼ cup aquafaba

½ cup dark brown sugar

1½ teaspoons vanilla extract

¼ cup molasses

1. Preheat the oven to 375°F. Prepare a muffin tin with liners.

2. In a small bowl, stir together the almond milk and cider vinegar. Let this sit until thickened and tangy, about 5 minutes.

3. In a large bowl, sift together the flour, baking powder, baking soda, and salt. Set aside.

4. Add the wheat bran to the milk mixture. Allow to stand for 10 minutes to soften the wheat bran.

5. In a separate bowl, stir the mashed banana, aquafaba, brown sugar, and vanilla together. Mix these wet ingredients into the wheat bran and milk mixture until combined. Pour this into the flour mixture and stir until a thick batter is made.

6. Scoop the batter into the prepared muffin tin and sprinkle with the raw sugar.

7. Bake for 15 to 20 minutes or until the muffins have puffed up and the tops are firm.

8. Brush the tops with molasses while hot.

9. Allow to cool for 30 minutes before removing from the tin.

YIELD: **12 muffins**   PREP TIME: **10 minutes**   COOK TIME: **15 to 20 minutes**

✳ Blueberry Muffins

In the summertime when fresh blueberries are in season, I like to bake with them as much as possible. Something about heating blueberries takes them from delicious to insanely luscious and tasty. They burst with juices when you bite into them. You can use frozen blueberries, but they will need to be tossed in ¼ cup of flour to help absorb any liquid they may release as they thaw. Feel free to substitute any berry (even cranberries, with orange zest instead of lemon) for your favorite variation.

2 cups all-purpose flour	1 teaspoon lemon zest
3 teaspoons baking powder	½ cup almond milk
½ teaspoon kosher salt	1½ teaspoons vanilla extract
½ cup Aquafaba Butter (page 128), softened	2¼ cups fresh or frozen blueberries
1 cup white sugar	1 tablespoon raw sugar
¼ cup plus 2 tablespoons aquafaba	

1. Preheat the oven to 375°F. Prepare a muffin tin with liners.

2. In a large bowl, sift together the flour, baking powder, and salt. Set aside.

3. Using a stand mixer or a hand mixer and a separate bowl, cream together the butter and sugar until light and fluffy, stopping and scraping down the bowl often.

4. With the mixer still running, slowly add in the aquafaba and lemon zest. If the mixture looks like it's about to break (when it gets grainy and the butter starts to separate), mix in a tablespoon of the flour mixture.

5. Once the aquafaba is mixed into the butter, add in half of the flour mixture, stirring only until combined. Pour in the milk and vanilla, and stir it until mostly combined. Add in the remaining flour mixture and blueberries.

6. Scoop the muffins into the prepared muffin tin and sprinkle with the raw sugar.

7. Bake for 30 to 35 minutes or until the muffins have puffed up and the tops are golden.

8. Allow to cool completely before serving.

YIELD: **12 muffins**   PREP TIME: **10 minutes**   COOK TIME: **30 to 35 minutes**

❋ French Toast

Use your own homemade Challah (page 108) to make this recipe even more satisfying. This recipe works great with slightly stale (think 1- to 2-day-old) bread. You can prepare this dish the night before if your bread is really dry; just let the bread soak in the mixture over night and make sure your skillet is extra hot, as the bread will be very soft.

1¼ cups aquafaba

½ cup coconut milk

1 teaspoon vanilla extract

½ teaspoon ground cinnamon

pinch kosher salt

¼ cup sugar

1 loaf French bread or Challah (page 108), cut into ¾- to 1-inch thick slices

2 tablespoons coconut oil

1. In a wide, shallow bowl, mix together the aquafaba, coconut milk, vanilla, cinnamon, salt, and sugar. Set aside.

2. Heat a medium to large skillet on medium high heat.

3. Dip as many pieces of bread as will fit in your pan into the milk mixture. Let set for about 30 seconds and flip.

4. Melt some of the coconut oil in the pan, and add the first round of toast. Cook until the bottoms are browned, about 3 minutes, and flip, cooking until both sides are browned. Set aside.

5. Repeat with the remaining slices, making sure to give each piece around 30 seconds in the milk blend so that the flavors get a chance to infuse throughout.

6. Serve with your favorite toppings.

YIELD: **12 to 14 slices**   PREP TIME: **10 minutes**   COOK TIME: **15 to 20 minutes**, depending on number of slices

✳ Carrot Lox

Pair this with your homemade AF Cream Cheese (page 125), some red onions, tomato, and of course, a perfectly toasted bagel. There are a few variations on carrot lox floating around these days, but I find that the aquafaba coating causes the carrots to adhere together and better re-creates the chew and texture of traditional lox.

1 tablespoon soy sauce

1 teaspoon liquid smoke

1 tablespoon dulse flakes

4 to 5 large carrots, thinly sliced lengthwise using a mandoline or peeler

⅓ cup aquafaba

1. Stir together the soy sauce, liquid smoke, and dulse flakes. Mix in the carrots and toss well to coat. Allow the carrots to marinate for at least an hour, tossing regularly to allow the carrots to leach out any excess liquid and get coated in the marinade. The carrots should be softened by the end of this time.

2. Preheat your oven to 350°F and line a baking sheet tray with parchment paper. Spray the parchment with nonstick cooking spray.

3. In a medium bowl, whisk the aquafaba until frothy. Drain the carrots from the soy sauce mixture, coat each strip in the aquafaba foam, and press the coated carrot out flat on the parchment. You want each carrot to slightly overlap the previous carrot, so that when they bake they stick together. You do not, however, want to just haphazardly toss these onto a tray; you want the entire batch to bake as evenly as possible. If there is any aquafaba left in the bowl after you've laid out all of the carrots, brush that on top of the spread-out carrots.

4. Cover the baking tray with aluminum foil. Bake for 30 to 35 minutes or until carrots are cooked through. Leave covered and allow to cool before storing in the refrigerator.

5. Serve on top of a toasted bagel with AF cream cheese (page 125) or as a topping for avocado toast. Also works great with mushrooms in crepes!

YIELD: about 1 pound lox   PREP TIME: 5 to 10 minutes, plus 1 hour to marinate
COOK TIME: 30 to 35 minutes

✳ Smoky Rice Paper Bacon

Once I discovered this bacon recipe, I knew I had to add it. It goes great with Cheddar Cheese (page 124) in the Savory Scones (page 119).

10 pieces rice paper	½ teaspoon liquid smoke
2 tablespoons aquafaba	½ tablespoon garlic powder
2 tablespoons nutritional yeast	½ teaspoon black pepper
3 tablespoons soy sauce	pinch hot pepper flakes, optional
1 teaspoon maple syrup	

1. Preheat your oven to 400°F and prepare two baking trays by lining them with parchment paper.

2. Take one piece of rice paper and brush it with water. Place another piece on top of the wet piece and rub them together so that they fuse. Repeat until all of the rice paper has been combined in two-piece stacks.

3. Using a pizza cutter or a pair of very sharp scissors, cut the rice paper into strips. Set aside.

4. Mix together the remaining ingredients in a wide, shallow bowl.

5. Dredge the strips of rice paper in the bowl of marinade. Place the marinated strips on the prepared baking trays.

6. Bake for 7 to 9 minutes, taking care to keep an eye on the strips, as they have a tendency to burn quickly. They are ready once they are crisped and browned.

YIELD: approximately 30 pieces of bacon   PREP TIME: 5 to 10 minutes   COOK TIME: 10 minutes

 # Quiche Crust

This recipe makes enough for a 9-inch quiche. I double this whenever I make it and freeze the second batch of dough. This recipe keeps in the freezer beautifully for 6 months.

1¼ cups all-purpose flour

1 teaspoon kosher salt

¼ teaspoon fresh ground black pepper

¼ pound Aquafaba Butter (page 128), cubed and cold

2 tablespoons aquafaba, refrigerated overnight

2 tablespoons vodka or white vinegar

1. In a large bowl, mix the flour, salt, and black pepper until combined.

2. Add the butter to the flour mixture and mix it all together until every piece of butter is coated with flour. Press each piece between your thumbs and fingers until you have flattened them all into flour-coated leaf shapes. This helps to make nice flakes, and working by hand helps to prevent overworking the dough.

3. Add the aquafaba and vodka or vinegar, and stir and squeeze the dough together with your hands until it's a shaggy dough that holds together. Wrap tightly in plastic wrap (if doubling, divide the dough in half before wrapping) and chill in the refrigerator for an hour. If not using immediately, place directly in freezer.

YIELD: 1 (9-inch) crust   PREP TIME: 10 minutes   COOK TIME: depends on the filling

✿ All the Greens Quiche

A rich, savory breakfast. This could be assembled the night before and baked in the morning.

1 Quiche Crust (page 27)

1 cup chopped red bell pepper

1 medium leek, white and light green parts only, sliced

5 cloves garlic, minced

1 cup kale, chopped

1 cup spinach, chopped

1 cup mustard or dandelion greens, chopped

¼ teaspoon fresh grated nutmeg

2 teaspoons kala namak salt

¼ cup aquafaba, refrigerated overnight

¼ teaspoon cream of tartar or 4 drops lemon juice

1 tablespoon soy sauce

3 tablespoons nutritional yeast

large pinch cayenne pepper

pepper, to taste

4 ounces silken tofu

1. Preheat your oven to 375°F. Line the bottom of a springform pan with parchment. Roll out the quiche crust to ¼ inch. Fill the springform pan with the dough running up the sides, but do not hang any dough over the top of the form. Dock the bottom of the quiche crust with a fork. Place in the refrigerator to chill for 30 minutes.

2. While the crust sets, prepare the filling. In a large, nonstick pan on medium-high heat, sauté the red pepper and leek, stirring occasionally until softened but not mushy, about 5 minutes. Add the garlic and cook, stirring nonstop for about 30 seconds. Remove these veggies from the pan and place in a large mixing bowl.

3. Wipe the pan out and return it to the heat. Add a small splash of water (2 tablespoons or so), and add the kale, spinach, and mustard greens. Add these in batches, if you must, until they are all in the pan. Cook the greens until they begin to wilt.

4. Add the nutmeg and kala namak salt to the greens and cook until there is no more liquid in the pan and the greens are completely soft. Add the greens to the bowl of peppers and leeks. Allow to cool completely.

5. Par bake the quiche shell for 15 to 20 minutes, or until golden. To do this, line the crust with parchment paper and fill with either dried beans or sugar and bake.

6. While the crust bakes, in a stand mixer, combine your aquafaba and cream of tartar or lemon juice, and whip on medium speed for about 5 minutes. You want to beat the aquafaba to stiff peaks, which means that when you remove the whisk, the tip of the peak holds its shape.

7. In a blender, combine the remaining ingredients until smooth. Fold this tofu mix together with the aquafaba.

8. Put the veggies into the prebaked quiche shell. Pour the aquafaba mix over the veggies and tap the pan to make sure the mix fills in all the nooks and crannies. Press it down with a spatula to smooth it out.

9. Bake for about 45 minutes or until the top is golden brown and set. Allow to cool fully before slicing. You can reheat it to serve.

YIELD: 1 (9-inch) quiche   PREP TIME:35 minutes, plus 30 minutes chill time
COOK TIME: 45 minutes

CAKE

A note on cakes: Aquafaba is a fantastic egg replacement, but it's important to remember that these two ingredients are not built the same way. Aquafaba cakes don't brown quite as drastically as cakes made with eggs. This means if you are new to vegan baking, you may have to check on your cakes sooner than you are used to, and the cake may be ready before it looks like it. Always use the touch or toothpick test. A cake that is ready should be springy and give back when gently pressed upon. A toothpick inserted into the cake should come out clean. If it doesn't, your cake needs more time. I'm also a huge, gigantic, over-the-top, feverishly devoted fan of cake strips. Cake strips are fabric liners that go around the outside of your cake pan and help the cake rise evenly (with less doming in the middle and a more even bake all around). You can make your own cake strips by using an old kitchen towel. Look online for a demonstration on how to make your own and use them for better cakes, every time.

There are recipes here for any type of cake or frosting that your heart may desire. Feel free to follow my suggestions or mix and match to suit your own tastes. Be sure to try making your own sprinkles. It's an easy project that's whimsical and easy in equal measure.

✳ Lemon Cake

This is the classic lemon pound cake, complete with glaze. This cake is perfect on a rainy afternoon with a nice cup of tea and some jazz radio.

1½ cups cake flour

2 teaspoons baking powder

¼ teaspoon baking soda

½ teaspoon kosher salt

1 cup vegan yogurt

½ cup aquafaba

1 cup sugar

zest of 2 lemons

2 tablespoons vegetable oil

LEMON SIMPLE SYRUP:

⅓ cup sugar

⅓ cup lemon juice

LEMON GLAZE:

1½ tablespoons lemon juice

¾ cup powdered sugar

1. Preheat your oven to 350°F. Allow the oven to preheat for 20 minutes while you prepare the cake. Spray an 8-inch loaf pan with nonstick spray. Line with parchment paper and spray again.

2. Sift together the cake flour, baking powder, baking soda, and salt into a large bowl. Set aside.

3. In a separate bowl, stir together the yogurt, aquafaba, sugar, lemon zest, and oil. Stir the yogurt mixture into the flour mixture until just combined, but no clumps of flour remain. Pour into loaf pan.

4. Bake for 50 minutes and check cake for doneness. If not done, cook another 5 minutes and check again. Repeat until done.

5. While the cake cooks, bring the sugar and lemon juice for the lemon simple syrup to a boil in a small pot. Boil for 5 minutes. Turn off heat and allow to cool.

6. Let the cake cool for 5 minutes before removing from the pan. Slide a dull knife or offset spatula along the edges, invert, and remove the cake from the pan. Brush cake liberally with the lemon syrup. Allow to cool fully.

7. To make the glaze, stir together the lemon juice and powdered sugar. Drizzle over the cake.

YIELD: 1 (8-inch) loaf cake   PREP TIME: 20 minutes   COOK TIME: 50 minutes

✳ Vanilla Sponge Cake

This is the very cake I think of when I think of a classic birthday cake. Try mixing in ½ cup of your Homemade Sprinkles (page 56) to make a confetti cake. This is a universal cake, and all frostings will go well with it. In this recipe, I specify imitation vanilla. You can use any vanilla you like, but imitation vanilla gives that nostalgic flavor that many of us in the States have grown up with. This cake is strong enough to make layers out of.

1½ cups cake flour

1 teaspoon baking powder

¼ teaspoon baking soda

pinch kosher salt

⅔ cup reduced aquafaba, refrigerated overnight

¼ teaspoon cream of tartar or 4 drops lemon juice

¾ cup sugar

1 teaspoon imitation vanilla extract

2 tablespoons vegetable oil

frostings and fillings of your choice

VANILLA SIMPLE SYRUP:

1 cup sugar

1 cup water

1 vanilla bean

1. Preheat your oven to 350°F. Allow the oven to preheat for 20 minutes while you prepare the cake.

2. Spray two 8-inch cake pans with nonstick spray. Line with parchment paper and spray again.

3. In a medium bowl, sift together the cake flour, baking powder, baking soda, and salt. Set aside.

4. Using a stand mixer, combine your aquafaba and cream of tartar or lemon juice, and whip on medium speed for about 5 minutes. You want to beat the aquafaba to soft peaks, which means that when you remove the whisk, the tip of the peak will collapse/fold over.

5. With the mixer still on medium, slowly sprinkle in the sugar. Continue to beat until the meringues are thick, shiny, and stiff peaked. Mix in the vanilla.

6. With the mixer still beating, slowly drizzle in the oil.

7. Gently fold in the dry ingredients, adding them in three batches.

8. Transfer the batter to the cake pans. Bake for 20 minutes and check cakes for doneness. If not done, cook another 5 minutes and check again. Repeat until done.

9. While the cakes cook, bring the sugar and water for the simple syrup to a boil in a small pot. Boil for 5 minutes. Turn off the heat and add the scraped insides of the vanilla bean. Reserve the leftover pod to make vanilla sugar.

10. Let the cakes cool for 5 minutes before removing from pans. Slide a dull knife or offset spatula along the edges, invert, and remove the cakes from the pans. Brush cakes liberally with the vanilla syrup. Allow to cool fully.

11. Before assembling layers, trim if desired, brush with syrup once more, and give the syrup 5 minutes to soak in. Top with desired frostings and fillings.

YIELD: 2 (8-inch) cakes   PREP TIME: 20 minutes   COOK TIME: 20 to 25 minutes

❋ Chocolate Sponge Cake

This light and airy cake is designed to be used in a layer cake but it can also be used in roulades (like the Yule Log on page 106), cupcakes, or sheet cakes. It's lighter than a Devil's Food Cake. Feel free to omit the rum in the syrup, but don't skip the coffee! Coffee supports cocoa and brings out the pure "chocolate" essence of this cake.

1¼ cups cake flour

¼ cup cocoa powder

1 teaspoon baking powder

¼ teaspoon baking soda

pinch kosher salt

⅔ cup reduced aquafaba, refrigerated overnight

¼ teaspoon cream of tartar or 4 drops lemon juice

¾ cup sugar

2 teaspoons vanilla extract

2 tablespoons vegetable oil

frostings and fillings of your choice

RUM SIMPLE SYRUP:

1 cup sugar

1 cup water

1 teaspoon instant coffee

2 tablespoons dark rum

1. Preheat your oven to 350°F. Allow the oven to preheat for 20 minutes while you prepare the cake.

2. Spray two 8-inch cake pans with nonstick spray. Line with parchment paper and spray again.

3. In a medium bowl, sift together the cake flour, cocoa powder, baking powder, baking soda, and salt. Set aside.

4. Using a stand mixer, combine your aquafaba and cream of tartar or lemon juice, and whip on medium speed for about 5 minutes. You want to beat the aquafaba to soft peaks, which means that when you remove the whisk, the tip of the peak will collapse/fold over.

5. With the mixer still on medium, slowly sprinkle in the sugar. Continue to beat until the meringues are thick, shiny, and stiff peaked. Mix in the vanilla.

6. With the mixer still beating, slowly drizzle in the oil.

7. Gently fold in the dry ingredients, adding them in three batches.

8. Transfer the batter to the two cake pans. Bake for 20 minutes and check cakes for doneness. If not done, cook another 5 minutes and check again. Repeat until done.

9. While cakes cook, bring the sugar and water for the simple syrup to a boil in a small pot. Boil for 5 minutes. Turn off the heat, add the instant coffee, and allow to cool. Once cool, stir in the dark rum.

10. Let the cakes cool for 5 minutes before removing from pans. Slide a dull knife or offset spatula along the edges, invert, and remove the cakes from pans. Brush the cakes liberally with the rum syrup. Allow to cool fully.

11. Before assembling layers, trim if desired, brush with syrup once more, and give the syrup 5 minutes to soak in. Top with desired frostings or fillings.

YIELD: 2 (8-inch) cakes   PREP TIME: 20 minutes   COOK TIME: 20 to 25 minutes

❋ Carrot Cake

It's hard to go wrong with carrot cake, a well-known crowd-pleaser. If you're feeling adventurous, try substituting parsnips for the carrots!

2½ cups all-purpose flour	¼ teaspoon ground ginger
3 cups grated carrots	¼ teaspoon ground nutmeg
1 teaspoon baking powder	¾ cup aquafaba
1 teaspoon baking soda	1 cup white sugar
½ teaspoon kosher salt	½ cup packed brown sugar
¼ teaspoon ground allspice	¾ cup applesauce
½ teaspoon ground cinnamon	Cream Cheese Frosting (page 45)

1. Preheat your oven to 350°F. Allow the oven to preheat for 20 minutes while you prepare the cake.

2. Spray a 9-inch cake pan with nonstick spray. Line with parchment paper and spray again.

3. In a medium bowl, sift together the flour, carrots, baking powder, baking soda, salt, and spices. Set aside.

4. In a separate bowl, whisk together the aquafaba, sugars, and applesauce.

5. Stir together the aquafaba and carrot mixture until just combined.

6. Bake for 40 minutes and check for doneness. If not done, cook another 5 minutes and check again. Repeat until done.

7. Let the cake cool for 5 minutes before removing from the pan. Slide a dull knife or offset spatula along the edges, invert, and remove the cake from the pan. Allow to cool fully.

8. To assemble, trim if desired, and top with Cream Cheese Frosting.

YIELD: 1 (9-inch) cake   PREP TIME: 20 minutes   COOK TIME: 40 to 60 minutes

✻ Apple Cake

I know this cake as "Jewish apple cake." At least, that's how it's been explained to me by my in-laws. My grandmother-in-law (or Baba-in-law) makes the best one I've had. I like to think that this one comes close.

¾ cup aquafaba

6 teaspoons ground cinnamon

5 teaspoons brown sugar

3 cups all-purpose flour

¾ teaspoon kosher salt

3 teaspoons baking powder

2 cups white sugar

1 cup applesauce

⅓ cup orange juice

1 teaspoon vanilla extract

6 small apples, peeled, cored, and chopped into chunks

1. Preheat your oven to 350°F. Grease an 8 x 8-inch square pan.

2. In a large bowl, whisk the aquafaba, cinnamon, and brown sugar together until smooth. Stir in the all-purpose flour, salt, baking powder, and sugar until just combined.

3. Gently stir in the applesauce, orange juice, and vanilla.

4. Scatter the apples over the bottom of the cake pan. Pour the batter over the apples and bake for 90 minutes, turning the pan 180 degrees at the halfway point. Cook until the top is set and golden brown.

5. Cool for 10 to 15 minutes before removing from the pan.

YIELD: 1 (8 x 8-inch) square cake   PREP TIME: **10** minutes   COOK TIME: **90** minutes

❋ Hazelnut Dacquoise

A dacquoise is a French-style cake. It's not as tall as the classic sponge cake, but thanks to the use of hazelnut flour, it's packed with flavor. If you use homemade hazelnut flour, roast the hazelnuts beforehand and make sure to sieve out any big pieces. Uniformity in the flour is important here.

2⅔ cups hazelnut meal/flour

¼ cup cornstarch

½ cup reduced aquafaba, cold

pinch kosher salt

¼ teaspoon cream of tartar or
4 drops lemon juice

¾ cup sugar

Chocolate Buttercream (page 41) or
Espresso Buttercream (page 40)

toasted crushed hazelnuts, to garnish, optional

1. Preheat your oven to 300°F. Allow the oven to preheat for 20 minutes while you prepare the cake.

2. Line a baking tray with parchment paper and draw three 8-inch circles on it.

3. Stir together the hazelnut flour and cornstarch in a small bowl and set aside.

4. Using a stand mixer combine your aquafaba, salt, and cream of tartar or lemon juice, and whip on medium speed for about 5 minutes. You want to beat the aquafaba to soft peaks, which means that when you remove the whisk, the tip of the peak will collapse/fold over.

5. With the mixer still on medium, slowly sprinkle in the sugar. Continue to beat until the meringues are thick, shiny, and stiff peaked.

6. Gently fold the hazelnut/cornstarch mixture into the aquafaba mixture. Fill the batter into a piping bag with a large tip.

7. Pipe out three 8-inch circles on the marked parchment. Spirals make beautiful designs, but artfully plated dollops are nice as well.

8. Bake for 1 hour, rotating every 20 minutes until the cakes are fully set but not browned.

9. Stack the layers and fill with complementary fillings like chocolate or coffee frostings. Garnish with the toasted crushed hazelnuts, if desired.

YIELD: 2 (8-inch) cakes   PREP TIME: 20 minutes   COOK TIME: 60 minutes

Swiss Buttercream

This luscious frosting is made from a base of meringue known as "Swiss meringue." In Swiss meringues, the traditionally used egg whites are heated with the sugar. This serves two purposes: to cook off any nasty bacteria in the raw egg whites and to dissolve the sugar. If you need a really white frosting, use clear imitation vanilla extract and add the smallest drop (or just dip a toothpick into a touch) of violet food gel coloring to offset any yellow tones from your vegan butter. Due to the cooking of both the aquafaba and the sugar, this buttercream is well suited for warm/humid weather, though that doesn't mean it's sun loving! Like any buttercream, this frosting likes to stay nice and cool. Keep in mind, you have to cook down the aquafaba and sugar mixture and allow them to cool completely overnight before getting started on this recipe.

1½ cups aquafaba

1 cup white sugar

¼ teaspoon cream of tartar or 4 drops lemon juice

¾ cup powdered sugar

1½ cups (12 ounces) solid Aquafaba Butter (page 128), cut into cubes and softened at room temperature

1 cup white vegetable shortening (or more butter if the cake does not need to withstand heat), cut into cubes and softened at room temperature

2 teaspoons vanilla extract

1. In a medium saucepan on medium-low heat, simmer the aquafaba until it has reduced to 1 cup, about 15 minutes.

2. Stir the sugar into the hot, reduced aquafaba and mix until the sugar as completely dissolved. Remove from the heat and refrigerate overnight until completely cooled.

3. Using a stand mixer, combine your aquafaba sugar mix with cream of tartar or lemon juice, and whip on medium speed for about 5 minutes. You want to beat the aquafaba to soft peaks, which means that when you remove the whisk, the tip of the peak will collapse/fold over. Continue to beat until the meringues are thick, shiny, and stiff peaked.

4. Reduce the speed to low and add the powdered sugar.

5. Beat in the butter and shortening, a few tablespoons at a time. Mix in the vanilla.

6. Use immediately. If not using immediately, store in the refrigerator. Make sure to bring this buttercream back to room temperature (no shortcuts! It MUST be completely at room temperature) and whip again before using.

YIELD: 5 cups PREP TIME: 20 minutes, plus an overnight rest COOK TIME: none

❀ French Buttercream

French-style buttercreams are not as glossy, heat resistant, or smooth as Swiss or Italian styles, but they are much quicker to whip up if you keep reduced aquafaba on hand. French buttercream is also softer and therefore not as well-suited for piping. If you don't have pre-reduced AF around, then remember you have to cook down the aquafaba and allow it to cool completely overnight before getting started on this recipe. If it's warm at all, the recipe will not work.

1½ cups aquafaba

1 cup white sugar

¼ teaspoon cream of tartar or 4 drops lemon juice

¾ cup powdered sugar

1½ cups (12 ounces) solid Aquafaba Butter (page 128), cut into cubes and softened at room temp

1 cup white vegetable shortening (or more butter if the cake does not need to withstand heat), cut into cubes and softened at room temperature

1 tablespoon vanilla extract

1. In a medium saucepan on medium-low heat, simmer the aquafaba until it has reduced to 1 cup, about 15 minutes.

2. Using a stand mixer, combine your aquafaba, sugar, and cream of tartar or lemon juice, and whip on medium speed for about 5 minutes. You want to beat the aquafaba to soft peaks, which means that when you remove the whisk, the tip of the peak will collapse/fold over.

3. Continue to beat until the meringues are thick, shiny, and stiff peaked.

4. Move the meringue to a different bowl.

5. In the mixer, combine the powdered sugar with the butter and shortening, using the paddle attachment until the butter mix is light and fluffy. Beat in the vanilla.

6. Remove the bowl from the mixer and, using a spatula, drop in ¼ of the meringue mix and stir this into the butter to loosen it. Continue to combine the two bowls by folding the meringue into the butter mixture, ¼ of the batch at a time, the same way you would mix together a mousse, until it is all combined.

7. Use immediately. If not using immediately, store in the refrigerator. Make sure to bring this buttercream back to room temperature (no shortcuts! It MUST be completely at room temperature), and whip again before using.

YIELD: 5 cups   PREP TIME: 20 minutes, plus an overnight rest   COOK TIME: none

❋ Chocolate Buttercream

A rich, dark chocolate take on the Swiss meringue buttercream. Keep in mind you have to cook down the aquafaba and sugar mixture and allow them to cool completely overnight before getting started on this recipe.

1½ cups aquafaba

1 cup white sugar

¼ teaspoon cream of tartar or 4 drops lemon juice

¾ cup powdered sugar

1½ cups (12 ounces) solid Aquafaba Butter (page 128), cut into cubes and softened at room temperature

1 cup white vegetable shortening (or more butter if the cake does not need to withstand heat), cut into cubes and softened at room temperature

4 teaspoons vanilla extract

1 cup (6 ounces) dark chocolate, melted and cooled

1. In a medium saucepan on medium-low heat, simmer the aquafaba until it has reduced to 1 cup, about 15 minutes.

2. Stir the sugar into the hot, reduced aquafaba, and mix until the sugar is completely dissolved. Remove from the heat and refrigerate overnight until completely cooled.

3. Using a stand mixer, combine your aquafaba sugar mix with cream of tartar or lemon juice, and whip on medium speed for about 5 minutes. You want to beat the aquafaba to soft peaks, which means that when you remove the whisk, the tip of the peak will collapse/fold over.

4. Continue to beat until the meringues are thick, shiny, and stiff peaked.

5. Reduce the speed to low and add the powdered sugar.

6. Beat in the butter and shortening, a few tablespoons at a time on medium-high speed. Mix in the vanilla and cooled melted dark chocolate on medium-high speed.

7. Use immediately. If not using immediately, store in the refrigerator. Make sure to bring this buttercream back to room temperature (no shortcuts! It MUST be completely at room temperature), and whip again before using.

YIELD: 5 cups   PREP TIME: 20 minutes, plus an overnight rest   COOK TIME: none

❊ Espresso Buttercream

Keep in mind you have to cook down the aquafaba and sugar mixture and allow them to cool completely overnight before getting started on this recipe.

1½ cups aquafaba

1 cup white sugar

¼ teaspoon cream of tartar or 4 drops lemon juice

pinch kosher salt

¾ cup powdered sugar

1½ cups (12 ounces) solid Aquafaba Butter (page 128), cut into cubes and softened at room temperature

1 cup white vegetable shortening (or more butter if the cake does not need to withstand heat), cut into cubes and softened at room temperature

1 teaspoon vanilla extract

3 tablespoons instant espresso powder, dissolved in 3 tablespoons warm water

1. In a medium saucepan on medium-low heat, simmer the aquafaba until it has reduced to 1 cup, about 15 minutes.

2. Stir the sugar into the hot, reduced aquafaba, and mix until the sugar is completely dissolved. Remove from the heat and refrigerate overnight until completely cooled.

3. Using a stand mixer, combine your aquafaba sugar mix, cream of tartar or lemon juice, and salt, and whip on medium speed for about 5 minutes. You want to beat the aquafaba to soft peaks, which means that when you remove the whisk, the tip of the peak will collapse/fold over.

4. Continue to beat until the meringues are thick, shiny, and stiff peaked.

5. Reduce the speed to low and add the powdered sugar. Beat in the butter and shortening, a few tablespoons at a time. Mix in the vanilla and dissolved espresso powder.

6. Use immediately. If not using immediately, store in the refrigerator. Make sure to bring this buttercream back to room temperature (no shortcuts! It MUST be completely at room temperature), and whip again before using.

YIELD: **5 cups**   PREP TIME: 20 minutes, plus an overnight rest   COOK TIME: none

❋ Fruit-Flavored Buttercream

Use this base recipe to make any fruit-flavored buttercream your heart desires. Fruit-flavored buttercreams tend to be much softer than their vanilla and chocolate counterparts; keep these babies refrigerated until ready to eat. Keep in mind you have to cook down the aquafaba and sugar mixture and allow it to cool completely overnight before getting started on this recipe.

1½ cups aquafaba

1 cup white sugar

¼ teaspoon cream of tartar or 4 drops lemon juice

½ cup powdered sugar

1½ cups (12 ounces) solid Aquafaba Butter (page 128), cut into cubes and softened at room temperature

1 cup white vegetable shortening (or more butter if the cake does not need to withstand heat), cut into cubes and softened at room temperature

1 teaspoon vanilla extract

½ cup fruit jam, pureed to a fine paste in the food processor

1. In a medium saucepan on medium-low heat, simmer the aquafaba until it has reduced to 1 cup, about 15 minutes.

2. Stir the sugar into the hot, reduced aquafaba, and mix until the sugar as completely dissolved. Remove from the heat and refrigerate overnight until completely cooled.

3. Using a stand mixer, combine your aquafaba sugar mix with cream of tartar or lemon juice, and whip on medium speed for about 5 minutes. You want to beat the aquafaba to soft peaks, which means that when you remove the whisk the tip of the peak will collapse/fold over.

4. Continue to beat until the meringues are thick, shiny, and stiff peaked.

5. Reduce the speed to low and add the powdered sugar. Beat in the butter and shortening, a few tablespoons at a time. Mix in the vanilla. Mix in the smooth pureed jam on medium speed.

6. Use immediately. If not using immediately, store in the refrigerator. Make sure to bring this buttercream back to room temperature (no shortcuts! It MUST be completely at room temperature), and whip again before using.

YIELD: 5 cups   PREP TIME: 20 minutes, plus an overnight rest   COOK TIME: none

 Royal Icing

Royal icing is a hard setting frosting that is used to ice cookies and add fancy, intricate decorations to cakes. If you are adding colors to your royal icing, make sure they are water- and not oil-based; the same applies with any flavorings. Oils will prevent the royal icing from setting/drying completely hard. A warm kitchen will make the royal icing take longer to set, so if your kitchen is warm, try popping the mixture into the freezer for a few minutes. Do not substitute lemon juice for cream of tartar in this recipe.

½ cup aquafaba

4 cups sifted powdered sugar, divided

¼ teaspoon cream of tartar

1 teaspoon clear imitation vanilla extract

water-based colors, optional

1. Using a stand mixer with the whisk attachment, beat the aquafaba with the cream of tartar until frothy, about 30 seconds.

2. Swap to the paddle attachment and add half of the powdered sugar to the aquafaba. Mix on low until combined.

3. Add the vanilla and remaining powdered sugar. Beat on low until combined and then turn up the mixer to medium high and beat for 5 minutes. If you are coloring the entire batch of royal icing, add any colorant now; otherwise, you can stir the color in smaller batches with a spatula.

YIELD: **3 cups**   PREP TIME: **7 minutes**   COOK TIME: none

✳ Cream Cheese Frosting

In my opinion, you can't have Carrot Cake (page 36) without cream cheese frosting. It's a nice tangy frosting that's at home on nearly any cake.

½ cup Aquafaba Butter (page 128), room temperature

1 cup AF Cream Cheese (page 125), room temperature

4 cups powdered sugar, sifted

2 teaspoons vanilla extract or vanilla paste

1. Beat together the butter and cream cheese until they are both combined, smooth, and fluffy.

2. Add in the powdered sugar, a cup at a time, and blend until completely combined.

3. Mix in the vanilla, and use immediately.

YIELD: **4 cups**   PREP TIME: **5 to 10 minutes**   COOK TIME: **none**

 # Gum Paste

Gum paste is used to make realistic edible flowers. Though they are edible, they are used for decoration, not snacking. Gum paste is a great asset to your cake-decorating repertoire. I learned this recipe from cake genius and pastry chef Nicholas Lodge in pastry school. Tylose powder is absolutely necessary for this recipe, and it can be found at many big-box chain stores like Michael's or Jo-Ann Fabrics. If neither of these are close to you, you can order it online. Do not substitute vegan butter or coconut oil for the vegetable shortening.

½ cup aquafaba

6 ⅔ cups powdered sugar, divided

gel coloring, optional

3 tablespoons tylose powder

1 tablespoon plus 2 teaspoons vegetable shortening, divided

1. Using a stand mixer with a paddle attachment, beat the aquafaba on high until frothy and loosened, about 5 to 10 minutes.

2. Reduce the speed on the mixer to low and gradually add in 6 cups of the powdered sugar. The mixture should be smooth and soft, like wet royal icing.

3. Turn the mixer speed up to medium and beat the mixture for 2 minutes.

4. The sugar mixture should resemble meringue at a soft peak stage, which is when you remove the mixer and the peak that is formed falls over onto itself. If you are adding color, this is when color should be added.

5. Reduce the speed to the lowest setting. Slowly sprinkle in the tylose powder. Count to 10 while you sprinkle it in to make sure you are not adding the tylose too quickly.

6. Turn the mixer up to the highest setting, and mix for a few seconds until the mixture is visibly thickened. Stop the mixer.

7. Scrape the paste out onto a table that has been sprinkled with some of the remaining powdered sugar. Use some of the shortening on your hands, about 1 tablespoon, and knead the paste, adding as much of the remaining powdered sugar as you need to create a smooth soft dough that no longer sticks to your hands.

8. Place the gum paste in a resealable bag or wrap it tightly in plastic wrap. Place this into a second resealable bag. Rest the gum paste for 24 hours in the refrigerator.

9. When you are ready to use the gum paste, take it out of the fridge, let it come to room temperature, and knead in a little more of the shortening. You may not need the remaining 2 teaspoons, but if your gum paste feels dry, use it all. Use as desired.

10. Always keep the gum paste sealed with as little air in the bag as possible when not using. This will keep up to 6 months in the refrigerator or up to 1 year in the freezer, well wrapped.

YIELD: about 4 pounds   PREP TIME: 15 minutes, plus overnight rest   COOK TIME: none

CANDIES

Candy-making is one of the most technically demanding things in the pastry universe, but I also think candies can be the most fun to make. They don't usually require much time to prepare, and these recipes provide some of the highest "reward to effort" ratio of any in this book. When the recipe calls for a candy thermometer, please use one. A thermometer will make the difference between a total failure and the chin-lifting pride of your candies coming together perfectly.

❋ Marshmallow Fluff

Marshmallow fluff no longer has to come from a jar at the grocer's. Now, you can quickly whip up (literally!) this confection for homemade fluffernutter sandwiches, s'mores brownies, or as the basis of the fudges found in this book.

½ cup aquafaba, refrigerated overnight

¼ teaspoon cream of tartar or
4 drops lemon juice

½ cup sugar

1 teaspoon vanilla extract

pinch kosher salt

1. Place the chilled aquafaba and cream of tartar or lemon juice into the mixing bowl of your stand mixer and beat on medium speed until soft peaks form, 3 to 4 minutes.

2. With the mixer still running, sprinkle in the sugar and beat until stiff peaks form, another 3 to 4 minutes.

3. Add the vanilla and salt and whip on high for 1 minute.

4. Use within the same day. If saving overnight, this fluff has a tendency to separate, but you can try to whip it together again.

YIELD: **2 cups fluff**   PREP TIME: **10 minutes**   COOK TIME: **none**

✳ Marshmallows

Marshmallows: You either love them or hate them. If your campfires have been missing s'mores for far too long, let aquafaba come to your rescue! This recipe calls for xanthan gum and agar agar powder, both of which can be found at health food stores and are necessary for this recipe. The aquafaba in this recipe is reduced in advance and chilled overnight. This recipe is inspired by the vegan food wizard Mihl, who runs the blog Seitan Is My Motor.

2 teaspoons agar agar powder

1 cup water, divided

1 cup white sugar

⅓ cup light corn syrup

½ cup aquafaba, reduced from
¾ cup and refrigerated overnight

¼ teaspoon cream of tartar or
4 drops of lemon juice

¼ teaspoon xanthan gum

2 teaspoons vanilla extract

1 cup powdered sugar

1 cup cornstarch

1. Combine the agar agar with ½ cup of water and allow it to dissolve in a small saucepan.

2. Lightly oil an 8 x 8-inch baking dish with nonstick spray.

3. In a medium saucepan, combine the sugar, ½ cup water, and light corn syrup. Cook on medium heat, stirring occasionally until the sugar is dissolved. Once the sugar mix is dissolved, turn the heat up to medium high, and do not stir anymore, as this can lead to the sugars crystallizing. Cook the sugar until it registers a temperature of 244°F on a candy thermometer.

4. Once the sugar syrup is nearly done, around 240°F, bring the agar agar and ½ cup water to a boil and allow to cook for 1 minute, without stirring.

5. While the sugar syrup is heating, whisk the aquafaba with the cream of tartar or lemon juice and xanthan in the bowl of a stand mixer on medium speed until you have stiff peaks.

6. Once the sugar syrup has reached 244°F (also known as the firm ball stage), turn the speed of the mixer up to high and slowly pour in the syrup in a thin but steady stream. Continue to whip the aquafaba with the syrup until the mix is light, pale, fluffy and has stiff peaks, 2 to 3 minutes.

7. With the beater still running, slowly add in the hot agar mixture and vanilla and beat another 5 to 10 minutes, or until you have a ribbon stage, and the marshmallow mix has begun to cool down but is still slightly warm. (The ribbon stage is when the mixture does not immediately melt back into the bowl when pulled away.)

8. While the marshmallow mixture is beating, combine the powdered sugar and cornstarch in a separate bowl. Sprinkle enough to coat the bottom of the greased 8 x 8-inch pan.

9. Pour the marshmallow mix into the prepared pan and using a greased spatula, try to smooth it out as smooth as possible.

10. Cool overnight on the counter. Sprinkle the top with the sugar/starch blend and cut using kitchen sheers into the desired size. Toss these pieces in more sugar/starch and store in an airtight container.

YIELD: 1 (8 x 8-inch) pan   PREP TIME: 5 to 10 minutes   COOK TIME: 20 minutes

✳ Fluffernutter Fudge

True fudge looks like it would be deceptively easy to make. While not technically difficult, there is a lot more going on in a bar of fudge than you might expect. Non-vegan versions often call for sweetened condensed milk, and in this recipe, we mimic that by cooking down our almond milk with some sugar. Traditionally, fudge is cooked to around 234°F, but I find cooking it to 244°F helps to counteract any softening from the homemade Marshmallow Fluff (page 49). If you prefer your fudge to be more meltingly soft, cook to 234°F instead.

2 cups sugar, divided

1 cup almond milk

½ cup Aquafaba Butter (page 128)

1¾ cups Marshmallow Fluff (page 49)

½ teaspoon kosher salt

8 ounces peanut butter (smooth or chunky)

1. Line an 8 x 8-inch pan with parchment paper and spray it with nonstick spray, or lightly oil the paper.

2. In a small saucepan, mix ¼ cup of the sugar and the almond milk. Bring to a boil, stirring frequently. Once boiling, reduce the heat and simmer, stirring occasionally until you have ½ cup of condensed sweetened almond milk. If you take this too far, you can mix in just enough water to equal ½ cup, and bring it back up to a boil once.

3. In a medium pot, melt the vegan butter and add in the remaining sugar and the condensed almond milk. Cook on medium heat, stirring occasionally until the sugar is dissolved. Once the sugar mix is dissolved, turn the heat up to medium high, and do not stir anymore, as this can lead to the sugars crystallizing. Cook the sugar until it registers a temperature of 244°F on a candy thermometer. Remove the syrup from the heat.

4. Stir in the marshmallow fluff, salt, and the peanut butter until they are totally combined. Transfer ingredients to the lined pan.

5. Allow to cool for an hour or so until the top is set. Cut into squares. Do this before it has completely cooled.

6. If your fudge is not setting as firmly as you'd like, try storing it in the refrigerator.

YIELD: 1 (8 x 8-inch) pan   PREP TIME: 5 minutes   COOK TIME: 25 to 30 minutes

Chocolate Fudge

This fudge is made using the same method as the Fluffernutter Fudge (see previous page) but results in a rich, chocolaty fudge. This is an instant favorite, as it's hard to find a more classic fudge flavor than chocolate.

1¾ cups sugar, divided

1 cup almond milk

½ cup Aquafaba Butter (page 128)

8 ounces dark chocolate, melted and warm

1¾ cups Marshmallow Fluff (page 49)

1 teaspoon instant espresso powder, dissolved in 2 teaspoons water

1. Line an 8 x 8-inch pan with parchment paper and spray it with nonstick spray, or lightly oil the paper.

2. In a small saucepan, mix ¼ cup of the sugar and the almond milk. Bring to a boil, stirring frequently. Once boiling, reduce heat and simmer, stirring occasionally until you have ½ cup of condensed sweetened almond milk. If you take this too far, you can mix in just enough water to equal ½ cup, and bring it back up to a boil once.

3. In a medium pot, melt the vegan butter and add in the remaining sugar and condensed almond milk. Cook on medium heat, stirring occasionally until the sugar is dissolved. Once the sugar mix is dissolved, turn the heat up to medium high, and do not stir anymore, as this can lead to the sugars crystallizing. Cook the sugar until it registers a temperature of 244°F on a candy thermometer. Remove the syrup from the heat.

4. Quickly stir in the melted chocolate. If the mixture begins to seize up, place it back on the heat briefly, stirring nonstop until the chocolate is completely mixed in.

5. Fold in the Marshmallow Fluff and the espresso powder until it is totally combined. Transfer ingredients to the lined pan.

6. Allow to cool for an hour or so until the top is set. Cut into squares. Do this before it has completely cooled.

7. If your fudge is not setting up as firmly as you'd like, try storing it in the refrigerator.

YIELD: 1 (8 x 8-inch) pan PREP TIME: 5 minutes COOK TIME: 25 to 30 minutes

 # Divinity

Divinity is the classic nougat-like confection that seems to be especially popular in the American South. Think of a cross between fudge and meringue. Feel free to mix in your choice of chopped add-ins (pecans are classic).

2½ cups sugar

½ cup water

½ cup light corn syrup

¼ cup aquafaba, refrigerated overnight

¼ teaspoon cream of tartar or 4 drops lemon juice

1 tablespoon natural vanilla extract

½ cup chopped, toasted pecans

1. Line a baking sheet or your counter with parchment paper. Lightly spray this parchment with nonstick spray.

2. In a medium saucepan, combine the sugar, water, and light corn syrup. Cook on medium heat, stirring occasionally until the sugar is dissolved. Once the sugar mix is dissolved, turn the heat up to medium high, and do not stir anymore, as this can lead to the sugars crystallizing. Cook the sugar until it registers a temperature of 260°F on a candy thermometer. Remove the syrup from the heat.

3. While the sugar syrup is heating, whisk the aquafaba with the cream of tartar or lemon juice in the bowl of a stand mixer on medium speed until you have soft peaks.

4. Once the syrup has reached 260°F (also known as the hard ball stage), turn the speed of the mixer up to high, and slowly pour in the syrup in a thin but steady stream. Continue to whip the aquafaba with the syrup until the mix is light, pale, fluffy, and has stiff peaks.

5. Mix in the vanilla and pecans, and spoon out drops of the Divinity onto the prepared parchment. Allow to cool before eating.

YIELD: about 36 drops   PREP TIME: 5 to 10 minutes   COOK TIME: 10 minutes

❋ Cranberry Pistachio Nougat

Nougat is a classic European confection, especially popular in Italy and France. Nougat keeps for so long that Italian American families in the Second World War would send out bars of the sweet treat to their sons fighting abroad. The nuts must be warm when added to the nougat mixture or else the mixture will seize up and become impossible to work with. You can do this by either re-warming the nuts (my preferred method, described below) or by toasting the nuts immediately before making the rest of the recipe and using the hot, toasted nuts.

¾ cup chopped, toasted pistachios

½ cup chopped, toasted almonds

¾ cup dried cranberries

2½ cups sugar

¾ cup water

2 cups light corn syrup

¼ cup plus 2 tablespoons aquafaba, refrigerated overnight

¼ teaspoon cream of tartar or 4 drops lemon juice

1 tablespoon vanilla extract

1. Start preheating the oven to 250°F. Place the nuts and cranberries on a baking tray and leave them in the oven while it preheats and while you make the rest of the dish.

2. Lightly spray a 9 x 12-inch baking dish with nonstick spray. Line the bottom and sides with parchment paper and spray this with nonstick spray as well.

3. In a medium saucepan, combine the sugar, water, and light corn syrup. Cook on medium heat, stirring occasionally until the sugar is dissolved. Once the sugar mix is dissolved, turn the heat up to medium high, and do not stir anymore, as this can lead to the sugars crystallizing. Cook the sugar until it registers a temperature of 270°F on a candy thermometer. Remove the syrup from the heat.

4. While the sugar syrup is heating, whisk the aquafaba with the cream of tartar or lemon juice in the bowl of a stand mixer on medium speed until you have stiff peaks.

5. Once the syrup has reached 270°F (also known as the soft crack stage), turn the speed of the mixer up to high, and slowly pour in the syrup in a thin but steady stream. Continue to whip the aquafaba with the syrup until the mix is light, pale, fluffy, and has stiff peaks.

6. Mix in the vanilla, pistachios, almonds, and cranberries and spread out the nougat onto the parchment-lined baking dish. Top with more oiled parchment and allow to cool overnight before cutting into bars.

YIELD: 1 (9 x 12-inch) pan   PREP TIME: 5 to 10 minutes   COOK TIME: 20 minutes

❋ Homemade Sprinkles

Sprinkles, jimmies, hundreds and thousands, whatever you like to call them, they've never been more popular! And now you can make a vegan version in any color or flavor that your heart desires.

3 cups Royal Icing (page 44), freshly made

water-based colorings, about 3-5 drops

¾ teaspoon water- or alcohol-based flavorings

1. Combine your royal icing, colors, and flavors. You will want ¼ teaspoon flavoring (if using an extract or liquor) for each cup of royal icing. You can make multiple colors at a time by mixing them into different bowls. The dried sprinkles will be a shade or two lighter than the wet royal icing, so make sure to color your mixture accordingly.

2. Turn a sheet pan upside down and line with parchment paper. Spray lightly with nonstick spray. Using a super-fine tip (think a Wilton #2 or #3) or my preference by far, a multi-use tip like a #134, fitted onto a pastry bag, pipe thin but constant lines of icing out onto the parchment.

3. Allow to dry overnight and then break into tiny pieces and store in an airtight container.

YIELD: about 4 cups sprinkles   PREP TIME: minimal, plus overnight to dry   COOK TIME: none

MOUSSES, PIES, AND PLATED DESSERTS

This chapter covers a whole set of showstoppers, from frozen mousses to pies and pie crusts all the way to plated desserts like Eton Mess and pavlova. While these kinds of desserts may seem overwhelming, all of them are fairly easy, but some may take a bit of planning (to allow for nights spent in the freezer, etc). With only a slight bit of consideration, you can wow your friends, family, or Instagram followers with these stunning and delicious desserts.

 # Eton Mess

This is a great recipe for any less-than-perfect meringues you may have lying around. I got instantly hooked on the dessert while road-tripping through Ireland one summer. Crunchy nibbles of meringue suspended in whipped cream with a healthy amount of strawberries mixed in can't go wrong.

4 cups fresh strawberries, chopped

2 teaspoons lemon juice

2 tablespoons sugar

1 (14-ounce) can coconut cream, chilled

2 to 3 cups crumbled Aquafaba Meringues (page 75) (about 4 large or 8 small)

1. Place the strawberries with the lemon juice and sugar in a bowl. Toss to combine. This will coax the juices out of the strawberries. Set aside while you make the whipped cream.

2. In a medium to large bowl, using either a hand or stand mixer, beat the coconut cream until it is light and fluffy.

3. Using a spatula, fold in the meringues and half of the strawberries with their liquid. Divide this mixture into 4 glasses and top with the remaining strawberries and juice. Serve immediately.

YIELD: **4 servings**   PREP TIME: **5 to 10 minutes**   COOK TIME: none

 # Pavlova

Pavlova is a dessert that is believed to have been created in New Zealand. Named after a Russian ballerina, it is most commonly associated with Australia. If that's not enough to sell you, know that the combination of crunchy, light-as-air meringue mixed with a whipped cream (I prefer coconut) and topped with fruit is a dessert that is greater than the sum of its parts.

1 recipe Aquafaba Meringues, unbaked (page 75)

1 (14-ounce) can coconut cream, chilled

¼ cup powdered sugar

2 tablespoons jam (your favorite flavor)

1 cup fresh fruit (something that complements the jam), to serve

1. Preheat your oven to 200°F. Allow the oven to preheat for 20 minutes while you whip and shape your meringues, and then turn it off. Alternatively, if you have a dehydrator, you can dehydrate your meringues on a higher temperature and low fan speed.

2. Prepare a baking tray by lining it with lightly oiled parchment paper or a Silpat baking sheet. Form the meringues by either piping or dropping 4 large nests onto the prepared baking tray. If you are using a dehydrator, pipe or drop the meringues directly onto your dehydrator sheets.

3. Leave the meringues in the oven for 2 hours minimum, preferably overnight, until they are dried out and you can easily pick them up off the baking tray. They should retain their shape and sound hollow if tapped on.

4. Once the meringues are baked and cooled, whip the cream. On medium speed, using either a hand or stand mixer, beat the coconut cream with the powdered sugar until light and fluffy. Spread out evenly over the 4 meringue nests.

5. Stir 2 tablespoons of water into the jam until your jam is a loose, runny sauce. Pour this over the coconut cream.

6. Top with the fresh fruit and serve.

YIELD: 4 servings   PREP TIME: 20 minutes   COOK TIME: 2 hours, plus overnight cooling

 Sweet Pie Crust

This recipe makes enough for a single-layer 9-inch pie. If you need to make enough crust to cover the pie completely, double this recipe. Heck, I double this whenever I make it regardless and freeze the second batch of dough. This recipe keeps in the freezer beautifully for 6 months.

1¼ cups all-purpose flour

½ teaspoon kosher salt

3 teaspoons sugar

¼ pound Aquafaba Butter (page 128), cubed and cold

2 tablespoons aquafaba, refrigerated overnight

2 tablespoons vodka or white vinegar

1. In a large bowl, combine the flour, salt, and sugar until combined.

2. Add the butter to the flour mixture and mix it all together until every piece of butter is coated with flour. Press each piece between your thumbs and fingers until you have flattened them all into flour-coated leaf shapes. This helps to make nice flakes, and working by hand helps to prevent overworking the dough.

3. Add the aquafaba and vodka or vinegar, and stir and squeeze the dough together with your hands until it's a shaggy dough that holds together. Wrap tightly in plastic wrap (if doubling, divide the dough in half before wrapping), and chill in the refrigerator for an hour. If not using immediately, place directly in freezer.

YIELD: 1 single-layer (9-inch) pie   PREP TIME: 5 minutes

Lemon Meringue Pie

This classic pie brings memories of sunny summer skies. Make sure you use fresh lemon juice, not stuff that comes from a bottle, for this recipe.

1 recipe Sweet Pie Crust (page 60)

1 cup sugar

¼ cup cornstarch

¼ teaspoon kosher salt

juice and zest of 3 lemons or ½ cup lemon juice

2 tablespoons coconut milk

12 ounces silken tofu

1 recipe Aquafaba Meringues (page 75), made but not baked

1. Preheat your oven to 350°F. Prebake the Sweet Pie Crust for 15 to 20 minutes and allow to cool for 20 minutes.

2. In a blender, combine the sugar, cornstarch, salt, lemon juice and zest, coconut milk, and tofu. Blend until completely smooth. Pour into the cooled pie crust.

3. Bake the pie for about 45 minutes, or until the center of the pie has a little wiggle but the edges are firmly set. Allow the pie to cool completely.

4. Once the pie has cooled, prepare the Aquafaba Meringues and arrange in a large mound on the pie. Using a creme brulee torch, toast the meringue until golden brown all over. Serve.

YIELD: 1 (9-inch) pie   PREP TIME: **30 minutes**   COOK TIME: **45 minutes**

❋ Key Lime Mousse

Growing up in Florida, key lime pie was the one dessert I could expect to show up at every bake sale, school event, holiday, you name it. This recipe taps into those memories, with a light-as-air key lime mousse topped with graham cracker bits. If you cannot find key limes or bottled key lime juice, make a mix of half lemon and half lime juice.

zest of 2 limes

½ cup key lime juice

¼ cup sugar

1 teaspoon agar agar powder

½ cup aquafaba, refrigerated overnight

¼ teaspoon cream of tartar or
4 drops lemon juice

1 teaspoon vanilla extract

½ cup coconut cream

½ cup graham cracker crumbs

pinch kosher salt

2 tablespoons coconut oil, melted

1. In a small saucepan, combine the zest, juice, sugar, and agar agar powder. Bring to a boil and simmer for 1 minute. Set aside to cool completely.

2. Using a stand mixer, combine your aquafaba and cream of tartar or lemon juice, and whip on medium speed for about 5 minutes. You want to beat the aquafaba to soft peaks, which means that when you remove the whisk, the tip of the peak will collapse/fold over.

3. Continue to beat until the meringues are thick, shiny, and stiff peaked. Mix in the vanilla.

4. Stir together the lime mix with the coconut cream.

5. Using a large spatula, carefully fold the key lime mix into the meringues until it is completely combined. Be careful not to mix more than you need to; you want to keep the fluffy nature of this dish intact.

6. Divide evenly among four ramekins.

7. While the mousse sets, mix the graham cracker crumbs with the salt and coconut oil. Use your hands to squeeze this mixture together in clumps. Sprinkle these tiny graham boulders over the key lime mousses. Refrigerate for a minimum of 4 hours; alternatively, you can make these the night before you want to serve them.

YIELD: **4** servings   PREP TIME: **10** minutes   COOK TIME: **4** hours refrigeration

✳ Roasted Strawberry Mousse

Roasting the strawberries gives them a depth of flavor that is lacking when they are fresh. Think rich, jammy fruit that's then mixed into a light mousse base and served chilled. I like to serve mine topped with a healthy dollop of vegan whipped cream (preferably coconut).

2 cups strawberries, stems removed	½ cup aquafaba, refrigerated overnight
2 tablespoons sugar	¼ teaspoon cream of tartar or 4 drops lemon juice
1 teaspoon vanilla extract	vegan whipped cream, to serve

1. Preheat the oven to 350°F. Line a baking tray with parchment paper.

2. In a bowl, toss the strawberries together with the sugar and vanilla. Pour the berries out evenly onto the prepared baking tray.

3. Roast the strawberries for 30 minutes, stirring occasionally to prevent the berries from burning.

4. Transfer the berries and their juices to a blender and blend until smooth. Set aside until cool.

5. Using a stand mixer, combine your aquafaba and cream of tartar or lemon juice, and whip on medium speed for about 5 minutes. You want to beat the aquafaba to soft peaks, which means that when you remove the whisk, the tip of the peak will collapse/fold over.

6. Continue to beat until the meringues are thick, shiny, and stiff peaked.

7. Using a large spatula, carefully fold the strawberry puree into the aquafaba mixture until it is completely combined. Be careful not to mix more than you need to; you want to keep the fluffy nature of this dish intact.

8. Divide evenly between 2 ramekins and refrigerate for a minimum of 4 hours; alternatively, you can make these the night before you want to serve them.

9. Serve with a dollop of freshly whipped vegan cream.

YIELD: **2 servings**   PREP TIME: **60 minutes**   COOK TIME: **4 hours refrigeration**

❄ Chocolate Mousse

This chocolate mousse whips up rather quickly and effortlessly. In fact, the hardest part of this recipe is waiting while it sets in the refrigerator!

½ cup aquafaba, refrigerated overnight

¼ teaspoon cream of tartar or
4 drops lemon juice

2½ ounces dark chocolate, chopped

1 tablespoon sugar

1 teaspoon natural vanilla extract

1. Using a stand mixer, combine your aquafaba and cream of tartar or lemon juice, and whip on medium speed for about 5 minutes. You want to beat the aquafaba to soft peaks, which means that when you remove the whisk, the tip of the peak will collapse/fold over.

2. While the aquafaba is mixing, place the chopped chocolate in a small microwave-safe bowl and microwave in 15-second bursts, stirring after each, until all of the chocolate is just melted, but not hot. Set aside until it is cool to the touch.

3. With the mixer still on medium, slowly sprinkle in the sugar. Continue to beat until the meringues are thick, shiny, and stiff peaked. Mix in the vanilla.

4. Using a large spatula, carefully fold in the melted dark chocolate until it is completely combined. Be careful not to mix more than you need to; you want to keep the fluffy nature of this dish intact.

5. Divide evenly among 2 ramekins and refrigerate for a minimum of 4 hours; alternatively, you can make these the night before you want to serve them.

YIELD: **2 servings**   PREP TIME: **10 minutes**   COOK TIME: **4 hours refrigeration**

✽ Peanut Butter Mousse

This recipe takes the chocolate mousse and ups the game with the addition of peanut butter. It's like a creamy, dreamy peanut butter cup with a definite grown-up flair.

½ can coconut cream

2 tablespoons creamy peanut butter

½ cup aquafaba, refrigerated overnight

large pinch kosher salt

¼ teaspoon cream of tartar or
4 drops lemon juice

2½ ounces dark chocolate, chopped

1 tablespoon sugar

1 teaspoon natural vanilla extract

¼ cup chopped roasted peanuts, for garnish

1. Using a stand or hand mixer, whip the coconut cream until light and fluffy.

2. Add the peanut butter and whip again until combined. This will be your peanut butter mousse layer. Set aside.

3. Using a clean bowl with your stand or hand mixer, combine your aquafaba, salt, and cream of tartar or lemon juice, and whip on medium speed for about 5 minutes. If your bowl is not clean and has any fat in it from the coconut or the peanut butter, your aquafaba will not whip up, no matter how long you beat it. You want to beat the aquafaba to soft peaks, which means that when you remove the whisk, the tip of the peak will collapse/fold over.

4. While the aquafaba is mixing, place the chopped chocolate in a small microwave-safe bowl, and microwave in 15-second bursts, stirring after each, until all of the chocolate is just melted, but not hot. Set aside until it is cool to the touch.

5. With the mixer still on medium, slowly sprinkle in the sugar. Continue to beat until the meringues are thick, shiny, and stiff peaked. Mix in the vanilla.

6. Using a large spatula, carefully fold the melted dark chocolate into the aquafaba mixture until it is completely combined. Be careful not to mix more than you need to; you want to keep the fluffy nature of this dish in tact.

7. Pour half of the chocolate mousse mixture evenly among four ramekins. Top the chocolate with a layer of the peanut butter mousse, and top this with the remaining chocolate mousse. Top with the chopped, roasted peanuts, if using, and refrigerate for a minimum of 4 hours; alternatively, you can make these the night before you want to serve them.

YIELD: **4 servings**   PREP TIME: **10 minutes**   COOK TIME: **4 hours refrigeration**

✳ Sweet Crepes

You will need a nice nonstick pan for this recipe. Don't fret if the crepes don't come out perfect on the first round! Everyone loses the first one or two. Feel free to serve these filled with any fruit; bananas and whipped coconut milk work exceptionally well.

⅔ cup aquafaba

1¼ cups all-purpose flour

¼ teaspoon kosher salt

2 tablespoons sugar

¼ to ½ cup almond milk, depending on thickness of batter

1 tablespoon coconut oil, melted

¼ cup vegan chocolate hazelnut spread, optional

1 cup chopped strawberries, optional

1. Whisk your aquafaba to break it up. It should start to froth up.

2. In a separate bowl, mix the flour with the salt and sugar.

3. Stir in the aquafaba, ¼ cup of almond milk, and coconut oil. The batter should be pourable and smooth, about the texture of coconut milk. Add more almond milk if needed.

4. Set your stove to medium-high heat. Coat a large pan or skillet with nonstick cooking spray. Let the pan get nice and hot.

5. Once the pan is hot, ladle a ¼-cup scoop of batter. Immediately use an off-set spatula, the back of a spoon, or simply a rapid swirling motion of the pan to spread the batter out into an even, thin circle.

6. Let the bottom of the crepe start to get golden brown, and flip carefully. The crepe should be ready to flip after about 30 seconds. Cook for another 30 seconds or until both sides are golden.

7. Stack the crepes on top of one another as you cook the rest; this keeps them soft and warm.

8. Optionally, spread the hazelnut spread on a center third of each crepe. Fold over twice into a triangular wedge and top with chopped strawberries.

YIELD: **about 10 crepes**   PREP TIME: **10 minutes**   COOK TIME: **15 minutes**

COOKIES

Cookies could be one of the main food groups. When I worked in a restaurant that served ice cream sandwiches, I ate at least one cookie a day, and probably an average of two or more! There is something just so perfect about the simplicity and portability of the cookie. I like to nibble on one when I have to do something less than pleasurable around the house, like paying bills. A spoonful of sugar, as they say. If you need a similar pick me up you'll find it here, whether your favorite cookie is actually a brownie, or perhaps a snickerdoodle, chocolate chip, or the classic French meringue.

❋ Chocolate Chip Cookies

What more can you say about chocolate chip cookies that hasn't already been said? I'd prefer to let these cookies speak for themselves. This recipe can easily be doubled.

½ cup Aquafaba Butter (page 128)

½ cup sugar

½ cup packed light brown sugar

1½ cups all-purpose flour

pinch nutmeg

1 teaspoon baking soda

½ teaspoon salt

3 tablespoons aquafaba

2 teaspoons vanilla extract

1 cup dark chocolate chips

flaky sea salt, for sprinkling

1. Using a stand mixer, beat the butter until it is smooth. Add in the sugars and continue to beat until the mixture is light and fluffy. Make sure to scrape down the sides of the bowl from time to time so that everything is blended well.

2. While the butter is beating, in a large bowl, stir together the flour, nutmeg, baking soda, and salt. Set this aside.

3. With the mixer on low speed, slowly add the aquafaba and vanilla to the butter and sugar mix. Mix this together until it's fully combined.

4. Add the flour mix to the butter mix, and stir by hand. Stir in the chocolate chips.

5. Let the dough rest for an hour in the refrigerator.

6. Preheat your oven to 375°F. Line a baking tray with parchment paper.

7. Scoop the cookies out, just shy of 2 tablespoons' worth, and flatten slightly. Sprinkle lightly with the flaky sea salt and bake for 10 to 11 minutes.

YIELD: 12 cookies   PREP TIME: 10 minutes, plus 1 hour refrigeration   COOK TIME: 10 to 11 minutes

✿ Sugar Cookies

If you're looking for a cookie to cut out and decorate, this is it. These cookies are designed to retain whatever shape they were before baking, so dust off those rolling pins and get festive!

½ cup Aquafaba Butter (page 128)

¾ cup sugar

1½ cups all-purpose flour

½ teaspoon baking powder

½ teaspoon kosher salt

3 tablespoons aquafaba

2 teaspoons vanilla extract

1. Using a stand mixer, beat the butter until it is smooth. Add in the sugar and continue to beat until the mixture is light and fluffy. Make sure to scrape down the sides of the bowl from time to time so that everything is blended well.

2. While the butter is beating, in a large bowl, stir together the flour, baking powder, and salt. Set this aside.

3. With the mixer on low speed, slowly add the aquafaba and vanilla to the butter and sugar mix. Mix this together until it's fully combined.

4. Add the flour mix to the butter mix, and stir by hand.

5. Let the dough rest for an hour in the refrigerator.

6. Preheat your oven to 375°F. Line a baking tray with parchment paper.

7. Lay down another piece of parchment or wax paper. Lightly flour it. Press down the cookie dough. Top with another piece of parchment and roll out the dough between the two sheets of paper. This makes returning the dough to the refrigerator much easier, if needed, and prevents the cookies from sticking. Cut out using cookie cutters. Make sure the dough stays cool at all times. Chill again for 15 to 20 minutes and then bake for 10 to 11 minutes.

8. If desired, decorate with Royal Icing (page 44) or any of the frostings in the cake chapter.

YIELD: about 24 cookies, depending on your cookie cutters   PREP TIME: 10 minutes, plus 1 hour refrigeration and 15 to 20 minutes to chill   COOK TIME: 10 to 11 minutes

❋ Snickerdoodles

Depending on where you grew up, you either know and love or have never heard of a snickerdoodle. Where the name comes from I have no idea, but it's a delightfully spiced and almost tangy cookie that will win you over if you've never had one before. Think of it as the valedictorian of the sugar cookie class. There are two types of snicks: cakey ones or chewy ones. If you like yours cakey, increase the baking time by 3 to 4 minutes, or until the tops of the cookies have cracked. If you like them chewy take them out of the oven when the center still looks a hint underbaked. Do not substitute lemon juice for cream of tartar in this recipe.

1 cup Aquafaba Butter (page 128)	2 teaspoons cream of tartar
¾ cup plus 2 tablespoons white sugar, divided	½ teaspoon kosher salt
¾ cup packed light brown sugar	3 tablespoons aquafaba
2½ cups all-purpose flour	1 teaspoon vanilla extract
1 teaspoon baking soda	2 tablespoons ground cinnamon

1. Using a stand mixer, beat the butter until it is smooth. Add in ¾ cup white sugar and the brown sugar and continue to beat until the mixture is light and fluffy. Make sure to scrape down the sides of the bowl from time to time so that everything is blended well.

2. While the butter is beating, in a large bowl, stir together the flour, baking soda, cream of tartar, and salt. Set this aside.

3. With the mixer on low speed, slowly add the aquafaba and vanilla to the butter and sugar mix. Mix this together until it's fully combined.

4. Add the flour mix to the butter and sugar mix and stir by hand.

5. Let the dough rest for an hour in the refrigerator.

6. Stir together the remaining 2 tablespoons of white sugar with the ground cinnamon.

7. Preheat your oven to 375°F. Line a baking tray with parchment paper.

8. Scoop the cookies out, 1 tablespoon at a time, and roll into a ball. Roll in the cinnamon sugar mix, and flatten slightly.

9. Bake for 8 to 10 minutes or until the tops are puffy and the edges golden.

YIELD: 24 cookies   PREP TIME: 10 minutes, plus 1 hour refrigeration   COOK TIME: 8 to 10 minutes

Peanut Butter Cookies

For this recipe I like to use the famous brand peanut butters, not the natural kind. You can make this recipe using natural peanut butter, or any other nut butter, but I like the nostalgic flavor of a brand like Jif or Skippy. The dough holds together better with these peanut butters. If you do use natural, you may have to up the flour by another couple of tablespoons.

½ cup Aquafaba Butter (page 128)

½ cup sugar

½ cup packed light brown sugar

1½ cups all-purpose flour

1 teaspoon baking soda

½ teaspoon kosher salt

3 tablespoons aquafaba

1 teaspoon vanilla extract

¾ cup smooth peanut butter

1. Using a stand mixer, beat the butter until it is smooth. Add in the sugars and continue to beat until the mixture is light and fluffy. Make sure to scrape down the sides of the bowl from time to time so that everything is blended well.

2. While the butter is beating, in a large bowl, stir together the flour, baking soda, and salt. Set this aside.

3. With the mixer on low speed, slowly add the aquafaba and vanilla to the butter and sugar mix. Mix this together until it's fully combined. Add in the peanut butter.

4. Add the flour mix to the peanut butter mix, and stir by hand.

5. Let the dough rest for an hour in the refrigerator.

6. Preheat your oven to 350°F. Line a baking tray with parchment paper.

7. Roll the dough into 1-inch balls, or a heaping tablespoon's worth. Press down with a fork and bake for 12 to 13 minutes.

YIELD: **24 cookies**   PREP TIME: **5 to 10 minutes, plus 1 hour refrigeration**   COOK TIME: **12 to 13 minutes**

❋ Peanut Butter Blondie

Despite my background in pastry, I've never been a big chocolate fan. Once I learned the wonders of black bean brownies, I knew a chickpea blondie had to be next. This is now in my go-to recipe realm. It's perfect for unexpected guests or sudden sweet cravings. Feel free to change the peanut butter chip for any kind of add-in that you like.

1 (15½-ounce) can no-salt-added chickpeas with brine or 2 cups cooked chickpeas and ⅔ cup aquafaba

½ cup sugar

¼ cup brown sugar

½ teaspoon baking powder

¼ teaspoon kosher salt

1 teaspoon vanilla extract

½ cup old-fashioned oats

¼ cup peanut butter chips

1. Preheat the oven to 350°F.

2. Using either a food processor or blender, combine all of the ingredients except for the oats and peanut butter chips. Blend well, stopping at least once to scrape down the sides of the blender carafe and blending again. You do not want any large chunks of beans in this batter. It should be very smooth.

3. Stir in the oats and peanut butter chips.

4. Pour the batter into an 8 x 8-inch glass baking dish.

5. Bake on the middle rack of the oven for 35 to 40 minutes, or until a knife poked into the center comes out clean.

6. Cool for at least half an hour before cutting and serving.

YIELD: 9 (1-inch) square blondies   PREP TIME: 10 minutes   COOK TIME: 35 to 40 minutes

✳ Black Bean Brownies

One of the wonders of AF is how it can be used to cut the oil in traditional recipes. This recipe is from my first book, Vegan Beans from Around the World. *I have updated it now to use AF in place of the oil, making this already-healthy indulgence even lighter! Just like the original, this recipe makes a fudge-like brownie. Make sure to use low-sodium or no-salt-added black beans for this recipe.*

1 (15½-ounce) can no-salt-added black beans with brine or 2 cups cooked black beans and ⅔ cup aquafaba

¼ cup sugar

¼ cup brown sugar

¼ cup plus 1 tablespoon cocoa powder (sifted if need be)

1 teaspoon baking powder

pinch kosher salt

1 teaspoon vanilla extract

1 teaspoon coffee (optional but worth it, can be left over from the morning)

1 teaspoon ground cinnamon

walnuts or dairy-free chocolate chips, for topping (optional)

1. Preheat the oven to 350°F.

2. Using either a food processor or blender, combine all of the ingredients except for the toppings. Blend well, stopping at least once to scrape down the sides of the blender carafe and blending again. You do not want any large chunks of beans in this batter. It should be very smooth.

3. Pour the batter into 8 x 8-inch glass baking dish. Add the toppings.

4. Bake on the middle rack of the oven for 20 to 25 minutes, or until a knife poked into the center comes out clean.

5. Cool for at least half an hour before cutting and serving. (If you can stand the wait. I had to eat a couple of hot and melty corners. I won't tell anyone if you do the same thing.)

YIELD: 9 to 12 brownies   PREP TIME: 10 minutes   COOK TIME: 20 to 25 minutes

❊ Hamantaschen

Hamantaschen is the classic cookie of Purim, but they are delicious any time of the year. The traditional fillings are poppy seed, apricot, and some type of red fruit, either raspberry, plum, or strawberry. Chocolate is also common. These cookies are adorable and fun to make, and they go fast!

2 cups all-purpose flour

1 teaspoon baking powder

¼ teaspoon kosher salt

⅓ cup sugar

¼ cup Aquafaba Butter (page 128), cubed and cold

¼ cup aquafaba

2 teaspoons vanilla extract

1 cup jam or three ⅓-cup denominations of different jams, for filling

1. In a large bowl, sift together the flour, baking powder, salt, and sugar.

2. Cut in the butter using a pastry cutter/dough blender or a couple of forks, or by pulsing the mix in a food processor. Mix until the dough resembles coarse sand.

3. Add the aquafaba and vanilla extract to the flour mixture and stir using a firm spoon or spatula. Stir until just combined into a rough dough.

4. Wrap the dough tightly with plastic wrap and rest in the refrigerator for at least an hour.

5. Preheat your oven to 375°F. Line a baking tray with parchment paper.

6. Roll the dough out to be ⅛-inch thick and cut out numerous circles, all the same size.

7. Place a small spoonful of jam in the center of each circle and pull up three sides of the circles until they create a triangular window that showcases the jam. Pinch together the edges where the dough meets. This keeps the cookies from opening up.

8. Bake for 16 to 18 minutes or until the edges are golden.

YIELD: about 24 cookies, depending on size of cutter   PREP TIME: 30 minutes, plus 1 hour refrigeration   COOK TIME: 16 to 18 minutes

Aquafaba Meringues

Meringues had long been an impossible dream for vegans. These naturally fat-free cookies are light as air while still being crunchy and sweet. An aquafaba classic recipe.

½ cup aquafaba, refrigerated overnight

¼ teaspoon cream of tartar or
4 drops lemon juice

¾ cup sugar

1 teaspoon vanilla extract

1. Preheat your oven to 200°F. Allow the oven to preheat for 20 minutes while you whip and shape your meringues, and then turn it off. Alternatively, if you have a dehydrator, you can dehydrate your meringues on a higher temperature and low fan speed.

2. Using a stand mixer, combine your aquafaba and cream of tartar or lemon juice, and whip on medium speed for about 5 minutes. You want to beat the aquafaba to soft peaks, which means that when you remove the whisk, the tip of the peak will collapse/fold over.

3. With the mixer still on medium, slowly sprinkle in the sugar. Continue to beat until the meringues are thick, shiny, and stiff peaked. Mix in the vanilla.

4. Prepare a baking tray by lining it with lightly oiled parchment paper or a Silpat baking sheet. Form the meringues by either piping or dropping dollops onto the prepared baking tray. If you are using a dehydrator, pipe or drop the meringues directly onto your dehydrator sheets.

5. Leave the meringues in the oven for 2 hours minimum, preferably overnight, until they are dried out and you can easily pick them up off the baking tray. They should retain their shape and sound hollow if tapped on.

YIELD: at least 24 (3-inch) meringues   PREP TIME: 20 minutes   COOK TIME: 2 hours to overnight to set

❋ Chocolate Pirouette Cookies

Once you've mastered the Ice Cream Cones (page 103) this will be a snap! The classic crème-filled pirouette cookie deserves to move out of the classic metal tin and into the repertoire of the home baker. Feel free to get creative with the flavors of the fillings and extracts. If you aren't a big chocolate fan, feel free to use the Ice Cream Cones recipe to make a vanilla (or lemon!) version. This recipe, like all tuile-based recipes, requires making a template. (Tuiles are a classic thin and crunchy French cookie often shaped like what most Americans would recognize as a Pringle potato chip. The name "tuile" is actually French for "tile.")

⅓ cup Aquafaba Butter (page 128)

⅓ cup powdered sugar

½ cup flour

1½ tablespoons cocoa powder, sifted if needed

2 tablespoons aquafaba

pinch kosher salt

1 teaspoon vanilla or orange extract

1 cup Chocolate Buttercream (page 41)

melted chocolate, for dipping, optional

1. Prepare the template. I like to use a flat plastic lid from a salad greens container, but you can also use a thin plastic cutting board or thin cardboard (think something like the front or back of a cereal box) if you don't intend to hold onto your template. Cut as many 5 x 3-inch rectangles as will fit on the piece of cardboard or plastic you are using, then discard the cut-outs and retain the outer area as your template. You will use the rectangular holes as your template.

2. Preheat your oven to 400°F. Using a stand mixer outfitted with the paddle attachment, beat the butter and sugar together on medium speed until well combined, about 2 minutes.

3. Change the speed to low and slowly beat in the flour until just combined. Add in the cocoa powder, aquafaba, salt, and extract. Once fully combined, stop the mixer.

4. Line a sheet tray with either a nonstick baking sheet (like a Silpat) or a lightly greased piece of parchment paper. Using an offset spatula, spread an even, but very thin layer, in the template on the paper or silicone sheet. Make sure you completely cover the inside of the template; no one wants holes in their tuiles! Gently pull away the template and repeat until your baking tray is full.

5. Bake in the upper half of the oven for 4 minutes. Rotate the tray and bake for another 4 minutes, or until the rectangles are a nice golden brown with a slightly pale center.

6. Remove from the oven and allow to cool for about 30 seconds before sliding the offset spatula underneath the tuile to loosen it from the tray. Using the handle of a wooden spoon, wrap the rectangle, lengthwise, around the spoon handle in a cylinder shape. They will start to set in seconds, so you will want to work quickly and work one at a time. The warm sheet tray will keep the others pliable. If they start to set while you are moving them, pop them back into the oven for 20 to 30 seconds.

7. Place the rolled cylinders into tall, thin glasses to cool.

8. Once completely cooled, use a piping bag to pipe the softened buttercream into the cookies. If desired, dip the cookies a quarter to halfway deep in the melted chocolate and set aside to cool. Store in an airtight container.

YIELD: about 24 cookies   PREP TIME: 5 to 10 minutes   COOK TIME: 10 minutes

MACARONS

Macarons are everywhere these days, and it's not hard to see why. These light and crunchy French cookies are perfectly portable (assuming you're only carrying one or two). Macarons are notoriously fickle, and it *will* take practice to get them where you want them. But no matter how they look, if you follow this recipe they will be delicious, though it may take time for you to perfect them. You can, however, take steps to ensure you're starting off on the best possible foot.

First, get your mise in gear! Mise, from *mise en place*, or French for "Get your stuff together," is step number one. You're going to want to have your oven preheated. I like to have my oven preheated for at least 20 minutes before I throw anything in there.

Before you get started, you're going to want to cut three pieces of parchment paper to fit your two baking sheets. Find yourself a nice cookie cutter about the size that you'd like the macarons to be. Using a permanent marker and said cutter, trace out circles on only one of the sheets where you are going to pipe your macs. Make sure to leave at least ¼ to ½ inch of space between them. Now, you are going to keep this paper safe, treasuring it and babying it so you can keep using it whenever you want to make macarons. Simply place another sheet of parchment on top of the designed one and pipe away. Then carefully slide out the bottom parchment and repeat with your second tray.

If you're new to the macaron game, I strongly advise against adding any colors or extracts until you get a feel for the process. Even gel-based colors change how wet the batter can be, and wet batters crack.

Macarons are weirdly better the second day, and even better still after having been frozen and thawed. Be careful with the freezing, however, if you are using something other than buttercream to fill them. Jam does not like to be frozen. If that's the route you are taking, you can freeze the shells themselves, defrost them, and fill them *a la minute* when you want to eat them, or you can skip the freezing altogether. Also, if you are freezing them they will keep indefinitely. Just make sure to wrap them well, as fat loves to absorb the flavor of anything nearby.

✿ Vanilla Macarons

The Parisian classic. For this recipe, you want to use the best vanilla extract you can find. If you have vanilla beans, scrape out the insides of 2 in place of the vanilla extract.

½ cup reduced aquafaba, refrigerated overnight

¼ teaspoon cream of tartar or
4 drops lemon juice

1¼ cups almond flour

½ cup powdered sugar

½ cup sugar

2 teaspoons vanilla extract

½ batch of your favorite Buttercream (page 39–page 43) or ½ cup jam, for filling

1. Using a stand mixer, combine your aquafaba and cream of tartar or lemon juice, and whip on medium speed for about 5 minutes. You want to beat the aquafaba to soft peaks, which means that when you remove the whisk, the tip of the peak will collapse/fold over.

2. In a separate bowl, sift together your almond flour and powdered sugar. If there are any large pieces left, discard these. Set aside.

3. With the mixer still on medium, slowly sprinkle in the sugar. Continue to beat until the meringues are thick, shiny, and stiff peaked. Mix in the vanilla. You want really stiff peaks to form on your meringue. In fact, you want this delicious fluff to get so firm that it forms a ball inside the whisk attachment of your mixer.

4. Now begins the most important step, called macaronage. Scatter the sifted flour mixture over the meringue, and using a large spatula, fold these in until just mixed. At first, the two mixtures will seem completely incompatible, but after 15 to 20 folds you'll see them start to mix. At this stage, the batter will be light and resemble a cloud, but the flour mixture and the meringue will be nowhere near mixed up entirely. Another 10 to 15 folds later, you should be at the proper texture, and the batter will be shiny, wet, and still thick. If you drop a piece of the batter into the rest, it will slowly spread out but won't fully melt back in. If the drop doesn't spread out at all then you need to mix more. If it melts back in immediately and won't hold any shape at all then you've over-mixed, and, well, there's not much you can do about that. Your best bet is to bake them off anyway and crumble them up as some kind of topping. Don't worry about being too gentle in this stage. You want to deflate the aquafaba a bit.

5. Once the batter is ready, pipe the macarons onto the parchment-lined trays. Tap the trays firmly on the counter at least 3 to 4 times, rotating the pan each time to knock out any large air bubbles. This step is very important; it helps prevent cracking and deflating later. Leave the macs to sit out for a couple of hours. Thirty minutes before they are ready to cook, preheat your oven to 300°F on an average day, of 275°F if it's really humid out.

6. Bake the macarons, one tray at a time, for 18 minutes or until the macs can be pulled off of the parchment without sticking. If they still stick, keep cooking for 1 to 2 minutes more until they cleanly come off of the paper.

7. Allow to cool completely before filling. Wrap in plastic wrap and rest for 24 hours before serving.

YIELD: about 24 sandwiches   PREP TIME: 20 minutes, plus 2-hour rest   COOK TIME: about 40 minutes, or 18 minutes per tray, plus overnight rest

❋ Raspberry Macarons

The tart sweetness of raspberry pairs wonderfully with the soft crunch of the macaron. I prefer my jam to have seeds in it, as I think the crunch adds texture, but if you're not a fan, feel free to use seedless.

½ cup reduced aquafaba, refrigerated overnight

¼ teaspoon cream of tartar or
4 drops lemon juice

1¼ cups almond flour

½ cup powdered sugar

½ cup sugar

2 teaspoons vanilla extract

3 to 5 drops red gel food coloring, optional

½ cup freeze-dried raspberries,
crushed to a powder, divided

½ cup raspberry jam, for filling

1. Using a stand mixer, combine your aquafaba and cream of tartar or lemon juice, and whip on medium speed for about 5 minutes. You want to beat the aquafaba to soft peaks, which means that when you remove the whisk, the tip of the peak will collapse/fold over.

2. In a separate bowl, sift together your almond flour and powdered sugar. If there are any large pieces left, discard these. Set aside.

3. With the mixer still on medium, slowly sprinkle in the sugar. Continue to beat until the meringues are thick, shiny, and stiff peaked. Mix in the vanilla. You want really stiff peaks to form on your meringue. In fact, you want this delicious fluff to get so firm that it forms a ball inside the whisk attachment of your mixer. Add the red gel food coloring, if using, and mix until just combined.

4. Now begins the most important step, called macaronage. Scatter the sifted flour mixture over the meringue, and using a large spatula, fold these in until just mixed. At first, the two mixtures will seem completely incompatible, but after 15 to 20 folds, you'll see them start to mix. At this stage, the batter will be light and resemble a cloud, but you will see the flour mixture and the meringue will be nowhere near mixed up entirely. Add ¼ cup of the powdered dried raspberries, and continue to mix. Another 10 to 15 folds later, you should be at the proper texture, and the batter will be shiny, wet, and still thick. If you drop a piece of the batter into the rest, it will slowly spread out but won't fully melt back in. If the drop doesn't spread out at all then you need to mix more. If it melts back in immediately and won't hold any shape at all, then you've over-mixed, and, well, there's not much you can do about that. Your best bet is to bake them off anyway and crumble them up as some kind of topping, like mentioned before. Don't worry about being too gentle in this stage. You want to deflate the aquafaba a bit.

5. Once the batter is ready, pipe the macarons onto the parchment-lined trays. Tap the trays firmly on the counter at least 3 to 4 times, rotating the pan each time to knock out any large air bubbles. This step is very important; it helps prevent cracking and deflating later. Sprinkle the macarons with the remaining powdered raspberries until they are covered. Leave the macs to sit out for a couple of hours. Thirty minutes before they are ready to cook, preheat your oven to 300°F on an average day, or 275°F if it's really humid out.

6. Bake the macarons, one tray at a time, for 18 minutes or until the macs can be pulled off of the parchment without sticking. If they still stick, keep cooking for 1 to 2 minutes more until they cleanly come off of the paper.

7. Allow to cool completely before filling with a thin layer of raspberry jam. Wrap in plastic wrap and rest for 24 hours before serving.

YIELD: about 24 sandwiches   PREP TIME: 20 minutes, plus 2-hour rest   COOK TIME: about 40 minutes, or 18 minutes per tray, plus overnight rest

✤ Hazelnootella Macarons

Chocolate and hazelnut, veganized and put into a delicate sandwich cookie. It's near impossible to eat just one.

½ cup reduced aquafaba, refrigerated overnight

¼ teaspoon cream of tartar or
4 drops lemon juice

1¼ cups hazelnut flour

½ cup powdered sugar

2 tablespoons cocoa powder

½ cup sugar

2 teaspoons vanilla extract

½ batch Chocolate Buttercream (page 41)
or ½ cup chocolate ganache, for filling

CHOCOLATE GANACHE:

1½ cups (12 ounces) full-fat coconut milk

10 ounces vegan dark chocolate

1. Using a stand mixer, combine your aquafaba and cream of tartar or lemon juice, and whip on medium speed for about 5 minutes. You want to beat the aquafaba to soft peaks, which means that when you remove the whisk, the tip of the peak will collapse/fold over.

2. In a separate bowl, sift together your hazelnut flour, powdered sugar, and cocoa powder. If there are any large pieces left, discard these. Set aside.

3. With the mixer still on medium, slowly sprinkle in the sugar. Continue to beat until the meringues are thick, shiny, and stiff peaked. Mix in the vanilla. You want really stiff peaks to form on your meringue. In fact, you want this delicious fluff to get so firm that it forms a ball inside the whisk attachment of your mixer.

4. Now begins the most important step, called macaronage. Scatter the sifted flour mixture over the meringue, and using a large spatula, fold these in until just mixed. At first, the two mixtures will seem completely incompatible, but after 15 to 20 folds you'll see them start to mix. At this stage, the batter will be light and resemble a cloud but you will see the flour mixture and the meringue will be nowhere near mixed up entirely. Another 10 to 15 folds later, you should be at the proper texture, and the batter will be shiny, wet, and still thick. If you drop a piece of the batter into the rest, it will slowly spread out but won't fully melt back in. If the drop doesn't spread out at all, then you need to mix more. If it melts back in immediately and won't hold any shape at all then you've over-mixed, and, well, there's not much you can do about that. Your best bet is to bake them off anyway and crumble them up as some kind of topping, like mentioned before. Don't worry about being too gentle in this stage. You want to deflate the aquafaba a bit.

5. Once the batter is ready, pipe the macarons onto the parchment-lined trays. Tap the trays firmly on the counter at least 3 to 4 times, rotating the pan each time to knock out any large air bubbles. This step is very important; it helps prevent cracking and deflating later. Leave the macs to sit out for a couple of hours. Thirty minutes before they are ready to cook, preheat your oven to 300°F on an average day, or 275°F if it's really humid out.

6. While the macs sit, make the Chocolate Ganache. In a medium saucepan, bring the coconut milk to a near boil. Remove from the heat.

7. Pour the heated coconut milk over the chocolate. Allow to sit for about 30 seconds. Whisk, starting in the center and staying there until the chocolate begins to become emulsified. Whisk until smooth and shiny.

8. Set the ganache aside, cover in plastic wrap, and refrigerate until firm, about 20 minutes.

9. Bake the macarons, one tray at a time, for 18 minutes or until the macs can be pulled off of the parchment without sticking. If they still stick, keep cooking for 1 to 2 minutes more until they cleanly come off of the paper.

10. Allow to cool completely before filling. Wrap in plastic wrap and rest for 24 hours before serving.

YIELD: about 24 sandwiches   PREP TIME: 20 minutes, plus 2-hour rest   COOK TIME: about 40 minutes, or 18 minutes per tray, plus overnight rest

❈ Pistachio Macarons

If you're making your own pistachio flour, make sure to toast your pistachios first by placing them on a baking tray and baking them in a 350°F oven for about 10 minutes, or until they are fragrant and taste lightly toasted. Allow to cool completely and grind into a flour using a food processor.

½ cup reduced aquafaba, refrigerated overnight

¼ teaspoon cream of tartar or
4 drops lemon juice

¾ cup almond flour

½ cup pistachio flour (or ground roasted pistachios)

½ cup powdered sugar

½ cup sugar

2 teaspoons vanilla extract

3 to 5 drops green gel food coloring, optional

½ batch of your favorite Buttercream (page 39–page 43) flavored with ½ to 1 teaspoon pistachio extract, for filling

1. Using a stand mixer, combine your aquafaba and cream of tartar or lemon juice, and whip on medium speed for about 5 minutes. You want to beat the aquafaba to soft peaks, which means that when you remove the whisk, the tip of the peak will collapse/fold over.

2. In a separate bowl, sift together your almond flour, pistachio flour, and powdered sugar. If there are any large pieces left, discard these. Set aside.

3. With the mixer still on medium, slowly sprinkle in the sugar. Continue to beat until the meringues are thick, shiny, and stiff peaked. Mix in the vanilla and the green gel coloring, if using. You want really stiff peaks to form on your meringue. In fact, you want this delicious fluff to get so firm that it forms a ball inside the whisk attachment of your mixer.

4. Now begins the most important step, called macaronage. Scatter the sifted flour mixture over the meringue, and using a large spatula, fold these in until just mixed. At first the two mixtures will seem completely incompatible, but after 15 to 20 folds, you'll see them start to mix. At this stage, the batter will be light and resemble a cloud, but you will see the flour mixture and the meringue will be nowhere near mixed up entirely. Another 10 to 15 folds later, you should be at the proper texture, and the batter will be shiny, wet, and still thick. If you drop a piece of the batter into the rest, it will slowly spread out but won't fully melt back in. If the drop doesn't spread out at all, then you need to mix more. If it melts back in immediately and won't hold any shape at all then you've over-mixed, and, well, there's not much you can do about that. Your best bet is to bake them off anyway and crumble them up as some kind of topping, like mentioned before. Don't worry about being too gentle in this stage. You want to deflate the aquafaba a bit.

5. Once the batter is ready, pipe the macarons onto the parchment-lined trays. Tap the trays firmly on the counter at least 3 to 4 times, rotating the pan each time to knock out any large air bubbles. This step is very important; it helps prevent cracking and deflating later. Leave the macs to sit out for a couple of hours. Thirty minutes before they are ready to cook, preheat your oven to 300°F on an average day, or 275°F if it's really humid out.

6. Bake the macarons, one tray at a time, for 18 minutes or until the macs can be pulled off of the parchment without sticking. If they still stick, keep cooking for 1 to 2 minutes more until they cleanly come off of the paper.

7. Allow to cool completely before filling with the pistachio-flavored buttercream. Wrap in plastic wrap and rest for 24 hours before serving.

YIELD: about 24 sandwiches   PREP TIME: 20 minutes, plus 2-hour rest   COOK TIME: about 40 minutes, or 18 minutes per tray, plus overnight rest

❧ Chocolate Earl Grey Macarons

One of the flavor combinations I learned in pastry school. This macaron is beyond sophisticated. These macs make wonderful, grown-up gifts.

½ cup reduced aquafaba, refrigerated overnight

¼ teaspoon cream of tartar or
4 drops lemon juice

1¼ cups almond flour

½ cup powdered sugar

2 tablespoons cocoa powder

½ cup sugar

2 teaspoons vanilla extract

Chocolate Earl Grey Ganache, for filling

CHOCOLATE EARL GREY GANACHE:

1½ cups (12 ounces) full-fat coconut milk

6 bags Earl Grey tea

10 ounces vegan dark chocolate

1. Using a stand mixer, combine your aquafaba and cream of tartar or lemon juice, and whip on medium speed for about 5 minutes. You want to beat the aquafaba to soft peaks, which means that when you remove the whisk, the tip of the peak will collapse/fold over.

2. In a separate bowl, sift together your almond flour, powdered sugar, and cocoa powder. If there are any large pieces left, discard these. Set aside.

3. With the mixer still on medium, slowly sprinkle in the sugar. Continue to beat until the meringues are thick, shiny, and stiff peaked. Mix in the vanilla. You want really stiff peaks to form on your meringue. In fact, you want this delicious fluff to get so firm that it forms a ball inside the whisk attachment of your mixer.

4. Now begins the most important step, called macaronage. Scatter the sifted flour mixture over the meringue, and using a large spatula, fold these in until just mixed. At first the two mixtures will seem completely incompatible, but after 15 to 20 folds, you'll see them start to mix. At this stage, the batter will be light and resemble a cloud but will can see the flour mixture and the meringue will be nowhere near mixed up entirely. Another 10 to 15 folds later, you should be at the proper texture, and the batter will be shiny, wet, and still thick. If you drop a piece of the batter into the rest it will slowly spread out but it won't fully melt back in. If the drop doesn't spread out at all, then you need to mix more. If it melts back in immediately and won't hold any shape at all then you've over-mixed, and, well, there's not much you can do about that. Your best bet is to bake them off anyway and crumble them up as some kind of topping, like mentioned before. Don't worry about being too gentle in this stage. You want to deflate the aquafaba a bit.

5. Once the batter is ready, pipe the macarons onto the parchment-lined trays. Tap the trays firmly on the counter at least 3 to 4 times, rotating the pan each time to knock out any large air bubbles. This step is very important; it helps prevent cracking and deflating later. Leave the macs to sit out for a couple of hours. Thirty minutes before they are ready to cook, preheat your oven to 300°F on an average day, or 275°F if it's really humid out.

6. While the macs sit, make the Chocolate Earl Grey ganache. In a medium saucepan, bring the coconut milk to a near boil. Remove from the heat and add the Earl Grey tea bags. Allow to steep for 10 to 15 minutes. Remove the tea bags and squeeze gently to remove the liquid. Don't squeeze too hard, or the tea will be bitter.

7. Pour the heated infused milk over the chocolate. Allow to sit for about 30 seconds. Whisk, starting in the center and staying there until the chocolate begins to become emulsified. Whisk until smooth and shiny.

8. Set the ganache aside, cover in plastic wrap, and refrigerate until firm, about 20 minutes.

9. Bake the macarons, one tray at a time, for 18 minutes or until the macs can be pulled off of the parchment without sticking. If they still stick, keep cooking for 1 to 2 minutes more until they cleanly come off of the paper.

10. Allow to cool completely before filling. Let the ganache come to room temperature and pipe to fill the sandwiches. Wrap gently in plastic wrap and rest for 24 hours before serving.

YIELD: about 24 sandwiches   PREP TIME: 2 hours 20 minutes (includes 2 hour resting)   COOK TIME: about 40 minutes, or 18 minutes per tray

ICE CREAM

Aquafaba ice creams have (rightfully) taken over as the best and easiest homemade vegan ice creams around. Ice cream made with aquafaba is decidedly fluffy. Think light and creamy.

There are two main kinds of aquafaba ice cream: Those made with a vegan, dairy-like coconut milk and those that are essentially sweetened, whipped aquafaba. They both have their fan base, so I have included selections of each.

The ones that don't call for any added milk get frozen as-is and tend to be icier, kind of like an ice cream that has melted partially and been frozen once more. If you're really, really in a pinch you can use ½ cup unreduced aquafaba in place of the suggested reduced ¼ cup, but this results in a much less "creamy" texture. You will also need to add stronger flavorings, as the fat in the coconut milk helps to mask any residual bean flavors. These recipes are absolutely the route to go if you're looking to cut out fat. Before serving, you will want to let these ice creams sit in the container at room temperature for 10 to 15 minutes to allow them to soften up slightly.

The recipes that include some kind of milk require an ice cream machine. The milk ones also require starting them the day prior. These recipes are truer to the classic ice cream but also take more work and time to make. They also have a hearty dose of fat and therefore do not need to be left out at room temperature to soften.

✳ Vanilla Ice Cream

This is the quick vanilla ice cream recipe. You will want to let this ice cream sit in the container at room temperature for 10 to 15 minutes before serving, to allow it to soften up slightly.

¼ cup aquafaba, reduced from ½ cup and refrigerated overnight

1 vanilla bean, scraped

pinch kosher salt

¼ teaspoon cream of tartar or 4 drops lemon juice

¾ cup sugar

2 teaspoons vanilla extract

pinch fresh nutmeg

1. Using a stand mixer, combine your aquafaba, scrapings from the vanilla bean, salt, and cream of tartar or lemon juice, and whip on medium speed for about 5 minutes. You want to beat the aquafaba to soft peaks, which means that when you remove the whisk, the tip of the peak will collapse/fold over.

2. With the mixer still on medium, slowly sprinkle in the sugar. Continue to beat until the meringues are thick, shiny, and stiff peaked. Mix in the vanilla and nutmeg.

3. Immediately pour this fluffed aquafaba into a freezer-safe container, either a quart container size or a standard loaf pan size.

4. Place in the freezer and cover the top with parchment paper and freeze for at least 4 hours before serving. The parchment paper helps to prevent iciness and freezer burn.

YIELD: about 1 quart   PREP TIME: 15 minutes   COOK TIME: 4 hours freezing time

❋ Vanilla Coconut Milk Ice Cream

This recipe may take a bit longer than the previous recipe, but the addition of the coconut milk makes a rich and creamy frozen dessert. This ice cream does not need to sit out before serving.

3 cups full-fat coconut milk

1 vanilla bean, scraped

¾ cup sugar

½ cup aquafaba

¼ teaspoon cream of tartar or
4 drops lemon juice

2 teaspoon vanilla extract

pinch kosher salt

1. In a medium saucepan, combine the coconut milk, scrapings from the vanilla bean, and sugar. Heat over medium high heat, stirring occasionally until the sugar has dissolved. Take the milk off the heat, transfer to a new container, and refrigerate overnight.

2. In a small saucepan (or the rinsed-out medium saucepan from before), heat the aquafaba on medium high heat until it boils. Lower the heat and simmer until it is reduced by half. You should now have ¼ cup reduced aquafaba. Take this off the heat and refrigerate overnight.

3. Using a stand mixer, combine your aquafaba and cream of tartar or lemon juice, and whip on medium speed for about 5 to 10 minutes. You want to beat the aquafaba to stiff peaks, which means that when you remove the whisk, the tip of the peak will hold its shape.

4. Gently fold the milk mixture into the fluffed aquafaba and immediately pour this into your ice cream maker. Follow the machine's instructions. The ice cream is ready to come out of the machine and head into the freezer when it resembles a soft serve consistency.

5. Place in the freezer and cover the top with parchment paper. Freeze for at least 2 hours before serving. The parchment paper helps to prevent iciness and freezer burn.

YIELD: 1 quart   PREP TIME: 20 minutes, plus overnight cooling   COOK TIME: varies, depending on your ice cream maker, plus 2 hours freezing time

Chocolate Ice Cream

This is the quick chocolate ice cream recipe, but technically it's more like a rich chocolate sorbet. You will want to let this ice cream sit in the container at room temperature for 10 to 15 minutes before serving, to allow it to soften up slightly.

¼ cup aquafaba, reduced from ½ cup and refrigerated overnight

pinch kosher salt

¼ teaspoon cream of tartar or 4 drops lemon juice

½ cup sugar

½ cup cocoa powder

⅛ teaspoon instant espresso

2 teaspoons vanilla extract

1. Using a stand mixer, combine your aquafaba, salt, and cream of tartar or lemon juice, and whip on medium speed for about 5 minutes. You want to beat the aquafaba to soft peaks, which means that when you remove the whisk, the tip of the peak will collapse/fold over.

2. With the mixer still on medium, slowly sprinkle in the sugar, cocoa powder, and instant espresso. Continue to beat until the meringues are thick, shiny, and stiff peaked. Mix in the vanilla.

3. Immediately pour this fluffed aquafaba into a freezer-safe container, either a quart container size or a standard loaf pan size.

4. Place in the freezer and cover the top with parchment paper. Freeze for at least 4 hours before serving. The parchment paper helps to prevent iciness and freezer burn.

YIELD: about 1 quart PREP TIME: 5 to 10 minutes COOK TIME: 10 minutes, plus 4 hours freezing time

✿ Chocolate Coconut Milk Ice Cream

A truer chocolate ice cream, as opposed to a chocolate sorbet, this recipe is rich, creamy, and has just the right amount of bitterness. The better the cocoa powder you use, the better the ice cream.

3 cups full-fat coconut milk

½ cup cocoa powder

¾ cup sugar

½ cup aquafaba

¼ teaspoon cream of tartar or 4 drops lemon juice

2 teaspoons vanilla extract

pinch kosher salt

1. In a medium saucepan, combine the coconut milk, cocoa powder, and sugar. Heat over medium high heat, stirring occasionally until the sugar has dissolved. Take the milk off the heat, transfer to a new container, and refrigerate overnight.

2. In a small saucepan (or the rinsed-out medium saucepan from before), heat the aquafaba on medium-high heat until it boils. Lower the heat and simmer until it is reduced by half. You should now have ¼ cup concentrated aquafaba. Take this off the heat and refrigerate overnight.

3. Using a stand mixer, combine your aquafaba and cream of tartar or lemon juice, and whip on medium speed for about 5 to 10 minutes. Add the vanilla extract. You want to beat the aquafaba to stiff peaks, which means that when you remove the whisk, the tip of the peak will hold its shape.

4. Gently fold the milk mixture into the fluffed aquafaba and immediately pour this into your ice cream maker. Follow the machine's instructions. The ice cream is ready to come out of the machine and head into the freezer when it resembles a soft serve consistency.

5. Place in the freezer and cover the top with parchment paper. Freeze for at least 2 hours before serving. The parchment paper helps to prevent iciness and freezer burn.

YIELD: about 1 quart   PREP TIME: 5 to 10 minutes, plus overnight refrigeration   COOK TIME: 10 minutes, plus 2 hours freezing time

✳ Espresso Ice Cream

Instant espresso gives off a much better flavor than traditional instant coffee. Instant coffee is not strong enough to give a true flavor. You will want to let this ice cream sit in the container at room temperature for 10 to 15 minutes before serving, to allow it to soften up slightly.

¼ cup aquafaba, reduced from ½ cup and refrigerated overnight

pinch kosher salt

¼ teaspoon cream of tartar or 4 drops lemon juice

¾ cup sugar

1 teaspoon vanilla extract

½ teaspoon instant espresso, dissolved in 1 tablespoon water

1. Using a stand mixer, combine your aquafaba, salt, and cream of tartar or lemon juice, and whip on medium speed for about 5 minutes. You want to beat the aquafaba to soft peaks, which means that when you remove the whisk, the tip of the peak will collapse/fold over.

2. With the mixer still on medium, slowly sprinkle in the sugar. Continue to beat until the meringues are thick, shiny, and stiff peaked. Mix in the vanilla and instant espresso.

3. Immediately pour this fluffed aquafaba into a freezer-safe container, either a quart container size or a standard loaf pan size.

4. Place in the freezer and cover the top with parchment paper. Freeze for at least 4 hours before serving. The parchment paper helps to prevent iciness and freezer burn.

YIELD: about 1 quart   PREP TIME: 5 to 10 minutes   COOK TIME: 10 minutes, plus 4 hours freezing time

❈ Espresso Coconut Milk Ice Cream

Instant espresso gives off a much better flavor than traditional instant coffee, which isn't strong enough. I love this ice cream served as an affogato, which is the Italian tradition of pouring a shot of espresso over a scoop of ice cream. Talk about being ready to dance the night away after dessert!

3 cups full-fat coconut milk

½ teaspoon instant espresso

¾ cup sugar

½ cup aquafaba

¼ teaspoon cream of tartar or
4 drops lemon juice

1 teaspoon vanilla extract

pinch kosher salt

1. In a medium saucepan, combine the coconut milk, instant espresso, and sugar. Heat over medium-high heat, stirring occasionally until the sugar has dissolved. Take the milk off the heat, transfer to a new container, and refrigerate overnight.

2. In a small saucepan (or the rinsed-out medium saucepan from before), heat the aquafaba on medium-high heat until it boils. Lower the heat and simmer until it is reduced by half. You should now have ¼ cup concentrated aquafaba. Take this off the heat and refrigerate overnight.

3. Using a stand mixer, combine your aquafaba and cream of tartar or lemon juice, and whip on medium speed for about 5 to 10 minutes. Add in the vanilla and salt. You want to beat the aquafaba to stiff peaks, which means that when you remove the whisk, the tip of the peak will hold its shape.

4. Gently fold the milk mixture into the fluffed aquafaba and immediately pour this into your ice cream maker. Follow the machine's instructions. The ice cream is ready to come out of the machine and head into the freezer when it resembles a soft serve consistency.

5. Place in the freezer and cover the top with parchment paper. Freeze for at least 2 hours before serving. The parchment paper helps to prevent iciness and freezer burn.

YIELD: about 1 quart   PREP TIME: 5 to 10 minutes, plus overnight refrigeration   COOK TIME: 10 minutes, plus 2 hours freezing time

✻ Strawberry Ice Cream

This is the quick strawberry ice cream recipe. This recipe is closer to a strawberry sorbet and has a brighter, more berry-rich flavor than the coconut milk counter part, but the texture is quite a bit denser. Before serving you will want to let this ice cream sit in the container at room temperature for 10 to 15 minutes to allow it to soften up slightly.

¼ cup aquafaba, reduced from ½ cup and refrigerated overnight

pinch kosher salt

¼ teaspoon cream of tartar or 4 drops lemon juice

1 cup frozen strawberries

½ cup powdered sugar

1. Using a stand mixer, combine your aquafaba, salt, and cream of tartar or lemon juice, and whip on medium speed for about 5 minutes. You want to beat the aquafaba to soft peaks, which means that when you remove the whisk, the tip of the peak will collapse/fold over.

2. While your aquafaba whips up. blend the frozen strawberries in a food processor until they are completely smooth. You can add up to 2 tablespoons of water to this if it is too thick to puree.

3. With the aquafaba mixer still on medium, slowly sprinkle in the sugar. Continue to beat until the meringues are thick, shiny, and stiff peaked.

4. Use ¼ of the whipped aquafaba and mix this into the strawberry puree to "loosen" the puree. Gently fold the strawberry mixture into the remaining aquafaba.

5. Immediately pour this fluffed aquafaba into a freezer-safe container, either a quart container size or a standard loaf pan size.

6. Place in the freezer and cover the top with parchment paper. Freeze for at least 4 hours before serving. The parchment paper helps to prevent iciness and freezer burn.

YIELD: about 1 quart   PREP TIME: 5 to 10 minutes   COOK TIME: 10 minutes, plus 4 hours freezing time

❋ Strawberry Coconut Milk Ice Cream

This recipe may take a bit longer than the previous recipe but the addition of the coconut milk makes a rich and creamy frozen dessert. Once the berries start appearing at the market and the sun starts to heat up, I know it's time to whip up this ice cream.

3 cups full-fat coconut milk

¼ cup sugar

½ cup aquafaba

¼ teaspoon cream of tartar or 4 drops lemon juice

pinch kosher salt

2 cups frozen strawberries

1. In a medium saucepan, combine the coconut milk and sugar. Heat over medium-high heat, stirring occasionally until the sugar has dissolved. Take the milk off the heat, transfer to a new container, and refrigerate overnight.

2. In a small saucepan (or the rinsed-out medium saucepan from before), heat the aquafaba on medium-high heat until it boils. Lower the heat and simmer until it is reduced by half. You should now have ¼ cup concentrated aquafaba. Take this off the heat and refrigerate overnight.

3. Using a stand mixer, combine your aquafaba and cream of tartar or lemon juice, and whip on medium speed for about 5 to 10 minutes. You want to beat the aquafaba to stiff peaks, which means that when you remove the whisk, the tip of the peak will hold its shape.

4. While this whips up, blend the frozen strawberries in a food processor until they are completely smooth. You can add up to 2 tablespoons of water to this if it is too thick to puree.

5. Use ¼ of the whipped aquafaba and mix this into the strawberry puree to "loosen" the puree. Gently fold the strawberry mixture into the remaining AF.

6. Immediately pour this into your ice cream maker. Follow the machine's instructions. The ice cream is ready to come out of the machine and head into the freezer when it resembles a soft serve consistency.

7. Place in the freezer and cover the top with parchment paper. Freeze for at least 2 hours before serving. The parchment paper helps to prevent iciness and freezer burn.

YIELD: about 1 quart   PREP TIME: 5 to 10 minutes, plus overnight refrigeration   COOK TIME: 10 minutes, plus 2 hours freezing time

❁ Mint Chocolate Chip Ice Cream

Green food coloring is optional in this quick mint chocolate chip ice cream recipe. Mint chocolate chip is always light, cool, and refreshing in a way most ice cream can only dream to be. You will want to let this ice cream sit in the container at room temperature for 10 to 15 minutes before serving, to allow it to soften up slightly.

¼ cup aquafaba, reduced from ½ cup and refrigerated overnight

pinch kosher salt

¼ teaspoon cream of tartar or 4 drops lemon juice

¾ cup sugar

1 teaspoon vanilla extract

½ teaspoon natural spearmint extract (peppermint can work but gives this a more candy cane flavor)

½ cup roughly chopped dark chocolate

3 drops green food coloring (optional)

1. Using a stand mixer, combine your aquafaba, salt, and cream of tartar or lemon juice, and whip on medium speed for about 5 minutes. You want to beat the aquafaba to soft peaks, which means that when you remove the whisk, the tip of the peak will collapse/fold over.

2. With the mixer still on medium, slowly sprinkle in the sugar. Continue to beat until the meringues are thick, shiny, and stiff peaked. Mix in the vanilla, mint, chopped chocolate, and green food coloring, if using.

3. Immediately pour this fluffed aquafaba into a freezer-safe container, either a quart container size or a standard loaf pan size.

4. Place in the freezer and cover the top with parchment paper. Freeze for at least 4 hours before serving. The parchment paper helps to prevent iciness and freezer burn.

YIELD: about 1 quart   PREP TIME: 5 to 10 minutes   COOK TIME: 10 minutes, plus 4 hours freezing time

✳ Mint Chocolate Chip Coconut Milk Ice Cream

This recipe may take a bit longer than the previous recipe but the addition of the coconut milk makes a rich and creamy frozen dessert. This is my go to nostalgia flavor. Nothing reminds me of family outings to the local ice cream parlor more than this minty green frosty treat.

3 cups full-fat coconut milk

¾ cup sugar

½ cup aquafaba

¼ teaspoon cream of tartar or 4 drops lemon juice

pinch kosher salt

1 teaspoon vanilla extract

½ teaspoon natural spearmint extract (peppermint can work but gives this a more candy cane flavor)

3 drops green food coloring, optional

½ cup roughly chopped dark chocolate

1. In a medium saucepan, combine the coconut milk and sugar. Heat over medium-high heat, stirring occasionally until the sugar has dissolved. Take the milk off the heat, transfer to a new container, and refrigerate overnight.

2. In a small saucepan (or the rinsed-out medium saucepan from before), heat the aquafaba on medium-high heat until it boils. Lower the heat and simmer until it is reduced by half. You should now have ¼ cup concentrated aquafaba. Take this off the heat and refrigerate overnight.

3. Using a stand mixer, combine your aquafaba, cream of tartar or lemon juice, and salt and whip on medium speed for about 5 to 10 minutes. You want to beat the aquafaba to stiff peaks, which means that when you remove the whisk, the tip of the peak will hold its shape. Mix in the vanilla, mint, and food coloring, if using.

4. Gently fold the milk mixture into the fluffed aquafaba and immediately pour this into your ice cream maker. Follow the machine's instructions. The ice cream is ready when it resembles a soft serve consistency. Once it reaches this point, add in the chopped dark chocolate and allow to mix until combined.

5. Place in the freezer and cover the top with parchment paper. Freeze for at least 2 hours before serving. The parchment paper helps to prevent iciness and freezer burn.

YIELD: about 1 quart   PREP TIME: 5 to 10 minutes, plus overnight refrigeration   COOK TIME: 10 minutes, plus 2 hours freezing time

❋ Rocky Road Ice Cream

Rocky road is the ice cream for people who like to take things up a notch; for those of you who don't just want their toppings on their ice cream, but inside it as well! Before serving, you will want to let this ice cream sit in the container at room temperature for 10 to 15 minutes to allow it to soften up slightly.

¼ cup aquafaba, reduced from ½ cup and refrigerated overnight

pinch kosher salt

¼ teaspoon cream of tartar or 4 drops lemon juice

½ cup sugar

½ cup cocoa powder

⅛ teaspoon instant espresso

2 teaspoons vanilla extract

½ cup toasted chopped almonds

½ cup Marshmallow Fluff (page 49)

1. Using a stand mixer, combine your aquafaba, salt, and cream of tartar or lemon juice, and whip on medium speed for about 5 minutes. You want to beat the aquafaba to soft peaks, which means that when you remove the whisk, the tip of the peak will collapse/fold over.

2. With the mixer still on medium, slowly sprinkle in the sugar, cocoa powder, and instant espresso. Continue to beat until the meringues are thick, shiny, and stiff peaked. Fold in the vanilla and chopped almonds.

3. Immediately pour this fluffed aquafaba into a freezer-safe container, either a quart size or a standard loaf pan size. Drop globs of the Marshmallow Fluff on top of the ice cream and swirl in using a butter knife.

4. Place in the freezer and cover the top with parchment paper. Freeze for at least 4 hours before serving. The parchment paper helps to prevent iciness and freezer burn.

YIELD: about 1 quart   PREP TIME: 5 to 10 minutes   COOK TIME: 10 minutes, plus 4 hours freezing time

✳ Rocky Road Coconut Milk Ice Cream

When plain old chocolate won't cut it, try this rocky road. This ice cream does not need to sit out before serving.

3 cups full-fat coconut milk

½ cup cocoa powder

¾ cup sugar

½ cup aquafaba

pinch kosher salt

¼ teaspoon cream of tartar or 4 drops lemon juice

1 teaspoon vanilla extract

½ cup toasted chopped almonds

½ cup Marshmallow Fluff (page 49)

1. In a medium saucepan, combine the coconut milk, cocoa powder, and sugar. Heat over medium-high heat, stirring occasionally until the sugar has dissolved. Take the milk off the heat, transfer to a new container, and refrigerate overnight.

2. In a small saucepan (or the rinsed-out medium saucepan from before), heat the aquafaba on medium-high heat until it boils. Lower the heat and simmer until it is reduced by half. You should now have ¼ cup concentrated aquafaba. Take this off the heat and refrigerate overnight.

3. Using a stand mixer, combine your aquafaba, salt, and cream of tartar or lemon juice, and whip on medium speed for about 5 to 10 minutes. You want to beat the aquafaba to stiff peaks, which means that when you remove the whisk, the tip of the peak will hold its shape. Mix in the vanilla.

4. Gently fold the milk mixture into the fluffed aquafaba and immediately pour this into your ice cream maker. Follow the machine's instructions. The ice cream is ready when it resembles a soft serve consistency. Once it appears ready, add the chopped almonds and mix until combined.

5. Immediately pour this soft serve into a freezer safe container, either a quart size or a standard loaf pan size. Drop globs of the marshmallow fluff on top of the ice cream and swirl in using a butter knife.

6. Place in the freezer and cover the top with parchment paper. Freeze for at least 2 hours before serving. The parchment paper helps to prevent iciness and freezer burn.

YIELD: about 1 quart   PREP TIME: 5 to 10 minutes, plus overnight refrigeration   COOK TIME: 10 minutes, plus 2 hours freezing time

❋ Ice Cream Cones

The hardest part of this recipe is cutting out the template, but once you've made it, you can reuse your template anytime. The batter for these cones is essentially a French tuile, or thin wafer cookie. Using the same template and an upside-down glass, you can make petite bowls to hold your sundaes.

½ cup Aquafaba Butter (page 128)	2 tablespoons aquafaba
⅓ cup powdered sugar	pinch kosher salt
¾ cup flour	1 teaspoon lemon, vanilla, or orange extract

1. Prepare the template. I like to use a flat plastic lid from a salad greens container, but you can also use a thin plastic cutting board or thin cardboard (think something like the front or back of a cereal box) if you don't intend to hold onto your template. Cut one or two circles about 5 inches in diameter into the plastic or cardboard, then discard the cut-outs and retain the outer area as your template. You will use the circular holes as your templates.

2. Preheat your oven to 400°F. Using a stand mixer outfitted with the paddle attachment, beat the butter and sugar together on medium speed until well combined, about 2 minutes.

3. Change the speed to low, and slowly beat in the flour until just combined. Add in the aquafaba, salt, and extract. Once fully combined, stop the mixer.

4. Line a sheet tray with either a nonstick baking sheet (like a Silpat) or a lightly greased piece of parchment paper. Using an offset spatula spread an even but very thin layer of batter in the template on the paper or silicone sheet. Make sure you completely cover the inside of the template; no one wants holes in their tuiles! Gently pull away the template and repeat until your baking tray is full.

5. Bake in the upper half of the oven for 4 minutes. Rotate the tray and bake for another 4 minutes, or until the circles are a nice golden brown with a slightly pale center.

6. Remove from the oven and allow to cool for about 30 seconds before sliding the offset spatula underneath the tuile to loosen it from the tray. Using either a cone-shaped roller, the end of a tapered French rolling pin, or a wooden citrus reamer, shape the tuile into a closed bottom cone. They will start to set in seconds, so you will want to work quickly and work one at a time. The warm sheet tray will keep the others pliable. If they start to set while you are moving them, pop them back into the oven for 20 to 30 seconds.

7. Place the rolled cones into tall, thin glasses to cool. Store in an airtight container.

YIELD: **16 cones**   PREP TIME: **5 to 10 minutes**   COOK TIME: **8 minutes**

 Baked Alaska

Baked Alaska is about as nostalgic a dessert as you can make, but it never ceases to impress.

3 cups Chocolate Ice Cream (page 93 and page 94), softened

3 cups Strawberry Ice Cream (page 97 and page 98), softened

½ Vanilla Sponge Cake (page 32), sliced thin to fit your bowl

½ cup aquafaba, refrigerated overnight

¼ teaspoon cream of tartar or 4 drops lemon juice

¾ cup sugar

1 teaspoon vanilla extract

1. Take a metal 5-cup-capacity bowl and spray it with neutral nonstick spray. Line the bowl with plastic wrap. Put a layer of Chocolate Ice Cream on the bottom. Place a layer of Strawberry Ice Cream on top of the chocolate. Repeat until there is only about an inch of space left at the top, doing your best to pack the ice cream down as solidly as possible. Press down with plastic wrap and place in the freezer until the ice cream is set solid, at least 2 hours but preferably 3.

2. Fill the empty space in the bowl with the sliced cake. Gently slide the ice cream out of the bowl, so the cake is on the bottom, and set on a plate. If you need to run some warm water over it to help that is fine, but it should just slide out with the plastic wrap. Leave this on a plate in the freezer.

3. Using a stand mixer, combine your aquafaba and cream of tartar or lemon juice, and whip on medium speed for about 5 minutes. You want to beat the aquafaba to soft peaks, which means that when you remove the whisk, the tip of the peak will collapse/fold over.

4. With the mixer still on medium, slowly sprinkle in the sugar. Continue to beat until the meringues are thick, shiny, and stiff peaked. Mix in the vanilla.

5. Fill the meringue into the piping bag and pipe over the round of ice cream. Use a torch to set the meringue. Serve immediately. Alternatively, you can bake this in a preheated 500°F oven for about 2 minutes.

YIELD: **1** dome   PREP TIME: **30** minutes, plus 2 to 3 hours to set   COOK TIME: **10** minutes

HOLIDAY SPECIALS

Just because these recipes are listed under "Holidays" doesn't mean you should relegate yourself to only making these once a year. I make challah often, and pumpkin pie finds its way into every fall and winter bake sale/pot luck/etc. that I attend. That being said, some of these recipes are "once a year" show-stoppers, like the yule log. Treat yourself, your family, and your friends this year with one of these holiday treats!

 Yule Log

Using recipes you've already mastered, you can whip up this fancy holiday classic.

1 recipe Aquafaba Meringues
(page 75) (unbaked)

1 recipe Chocolate Sponge Cake (page
34), batter mixed but not baked

1 recipe Chocolate Buttercream (page 41),
room temperature cocoa powder, for dusting

1. Prepare and bake the Aquafaba Meringues as stated in the recipe on page 75. Pipe into "stems," or mini logs, and rounds, or "mushroom tops." Bake according to instructions in recipe.

2. Preheat your oven to 350°F. Line a baking tray with parchment paper and spray with nonstick spray.

3. Pour the Chocolate Sponge Cake batter into the baking tray and spread out into an even, thin layer. You want the batter to be as evenly spread out as possible, taking the batter to the very edges of the pan.

3. Use your thumb to wipe a clean line between the edges of the baking tray and the batter inside. Bake in the middle of the oven for 10 minutes, rotating and baking another 10 minutes or until the top of the cake is set. Remove from the oven and allow to cool for 5 minutes.

4. Lay a clean, floured kitchen towel over the cake, and invert quickly to release the cake from the pan. Gently roll up into a roulade and set aside to cool. Cooling the cake in this shape makes it easier to work with later.

5. Unravel the cake carefully, and cover with a thick layer of Chocolate Buttercream. Roll the cake back up. Cut off ¼ of the cake, at an angle. Press this angle up against the side of the cake, creating a branch-like appearance.

6. Use a dot of frosting to connect a "mushroom top" to a "stem." Dust the "mushrooms" with a light dusting of cocoa powder.

7. Cover the exterior of the cake with the rest of the frosting. Use a fork dragged along the cream to give it a texture similar to bark.

8. Attach the "mushrooms" to the "log" and serve.

YIELD: 1 log   PREP TIME: 50 minutes   COOK TIME: 20 minutes

 # Egg Nog

Eggnog is typically made with a custard that is lightened with whipped egg whites. I've never been a big fan of the vegg nogs that are made with heavy coconut cream, tofu, or nut bases. They're too heavy to have more than half of a mug full of, at least for my taste. This recipe makes a lighter custard base using flour and almond milk and whips the custard up with the whites.

¼ cup flour	3 tablespoons sugar
1 cup almond milk	2 teaspoons vanilla extract
½ cup aquafaba, refrigerated overnight	pinch kosher salt
¼ teaspoon cream of tartar or 4 drops lemon juice	fresh ground nutmeg, to taste
	rum, brandy, or bourbon, to taste (optional)

1. In a small pan, whisk together the flour and almond milk. Cook over medium heat, whisking constantly to prevent/remove clumps. Once the mixture thickens, lower the heat and allow to cook, stirring occasionally to prevent the bottom from burning. Cook for about an additional 5 minutes or until the mixture no longer tastes of raw flour. Remove from heat and set aside until cool.

2. Using a stand mixer, combine your aquafaba and cream of tartar or lemon juice, and whip on medium speed for about 5 minutes. You want to beat the aquafaba to soft peaks, which means that when you remove the whisk, the tip of the peak will collapse/fold over.

3. With the mixer still on medium, slowly sprinkle in the sugar. Continue to beat until the meringues are thick, shiny, and stiff peaked. Mix in the vanilla and salt.

4. Loosen the custard with some of the meringue. Don't worry too much about deflating the meringue at this point. Add some fresh nutmeg to taste. Fold in the rest of the meringue until combined. Add in the liquor of your choice, if using; if not, you may need to thin the nog out with a little almond milk.

5. Serve immediately, topped with more fresh ground nutmeg.

YIELD: **4 cups**   PREP TIME: **10 minutes**   COOK TIME: **15 minutes**

# Challah

Challah is a classic bread that makes one heck of a French Toast (page 24). Challah is an "enriched dough," meaning there are more ingredients added to it (normally a lot of fat). This recipe uses aquafaba to get rid of the oil. If the dough tastes too "lean" to you after trying it this way, feel free to sub out the aquafaba that is in the dough for vegetable oil. Don't substitute the aquafaba for the gloss. Like any yeasted bread, this bread takes some time to rise, so don't try to rush it. Your patience will be rewarded. I call for instant dry yeast in this recipe, as it allows me to skip the proofing stage in the beginning. If you only have active dry yeast, help it to "wake up" by mixing it with ¼ cup of warm water and 1 tablespoon of sugar and allowing it to sit for 10 minutes or until the yeast foams.

¼ cup plus 2 tablespoons sugar	½ teaspoon kosher salt
1 tablespoon instant dry yeast	6 tablespoons aquafaba, divided
3 cups bread flour	sesame seeds, optional, for topping

1. In a stand mixer with the dough hook attachment, stir together the sugar, yeast, bread flour, and salt on low speed.

2. With the mixer still running, pour in 1¼ cups of warm water (about 105 to 110°F) and 3 tablespoons of the aquafaba. Once fully combined, turn speed up to medium.

3. Knead on medium speed for about 5 minutes or until you have a smooth dough.

4. Lightly oil a large bowl and place the dough inside. Cover loosely with oiled plastic wrap, then with a clean kitchen towel, and leave to rise somewhere warm (but not hot!) for about 1 hour or until your dough has doubled in size. If using active dry yeast, this may take up to 90 minutes. Go by the size of the dough, not the time passed.

5. Roll dough out onto a lightly floured surface. Gently deflate by folding the dough over twice and pressing out the air. Divide the dough into six even-sized balls. Roll each ball into a long snake with tapered ends. Braid three of the snakes together, pinching and tucking both ends under. Repeat with the remaining three portions of dough.

6. Turn a baking tray upside down and cover with parchment paper and place the two loaves on top. Alternatively, if you have a pizza peel, you can use that instead, lined with parchment paper.

7. Loosely cover the loaves with lightly oiled plastic wrap and let rise until doubled once more, about another hour.

8. Forty minutes before the loaves are ready, preheat your oven to 425°F. Position a rack in the middle of the oven.

9. Twenty minutes before baking the loaves, put a glass or metal baking dish filled with 3 to 4 cups of water (depending on the size of your pan) on the bottom of the oven. This creates steam that will make a better crust.

10. Once the loaves are ready to bake, remove the plastic wrap. Brush the loaves with the remaining aquafaba and sprinkle with sesame seeds, if using.

11. Use the baking tray like a pizza peel, and working quickly, slide the parchment and loaves directly onto the oven rack. Cook for 15 minutes.

12. Remove the water pan and lower the heat to 350°F. Cook for another 15 to 20 minutes or until the challahs are golden brown and produce a hollow sound when turned upside down and tapped on the bottom.

13. Allow to cool fully before slicing. Otherwise, the bread may not finish cooking all the way and will definitely be dry and stale.

YIELD: 2 loaves   PREP TIME: 10 minutes, plus rising time   COOK TIME: 35 minutes

 Pumpkin Pie

The holiday season just isn't the same without pumpkin pie. Sweet potatoes have a brighter, stronger flavor and combining the two makes a pie that tastes like how we all remember pumpkin pie to be growing up. That is, uniquely vegetal, sweet, and homey—never watery or bland. As much as I love "from scratch" baking, I've found that canned pumpkin puree is just the best ingredient to use. Home roasted doesn't give the same flavor. However, feel free to roast your own sweet potatoes. If you have pumpkin pie spice mix at home already, feel free to use 2 teaspoons of that in place of the spices listed. (Still use the salt, though).

1 recipe Sweet Pie Crust (page 60)	1 teaspoon ground cinnamon
½ cup aquafaba	½ teaspoon ground ginger
1 cup pumpkin puree	pinch ground cloves
1 cup sweet potato puree	pinch fresh ground nutmeg
⅓ cup sugar	¼ teaspoon kosher salt
2 tablespoons coconut oil, melted	whipped coconut cream, to serve

1. Preheat your oven to 350°F. Prebake your Sweet Pie Crust for 15 to 20 minutes and allow to cool for 20 minutes.

2. In a food processor, combine the aquafaba, pumpkin, sweet potato, and sugar. Blend until completely smooth. With the food processor still running, add in the coconut oil, spices, and salt. Pour into the cooled pie crust.

3. Bake the pie for about 40 minutes or until the center of the pie has a little wiggle but the edges are firmly set. Allow the pie to cool completely.

4. Keep stored in the refrigerator until ready to serve. Serve with whipped coconut cream.

YIELD: 1 (9-inch) pie   PREP TIME: 30 minutes   COOK TIME: 40 minutes

SAVORY TREATS

Baking is all sugary sweet. In this chapter, you'll find recipes for flatbreads, pizza, scones, cornbread, and even a mushroom pot pie. Savory baking is actually my favorite kind of baking. You can only eat dessert so often, but as it's been said, "give us this day our daily bread." I'm pretty sure they meant pizza. Toward the end of this chapter you'll find recipes to make your own cheese. They aren't technically demanding, but you will want to make sure you have all the ingredients you need because substitutions are hit or miss.

 # Pizza Dough

Use this pizza dough recipe to go with all of your homemade cheeses! I like Mozzarella Cheese (page 122) with fresh tomatoes and basil, or Cheddar Cheese (page 124) with sliced green olives and tomato sauce. You can use this dough recipe as a starting point for any of the flatbread varieties.

2¼ teaspoons instant yeast

1 tablespoon sugar

1 teaspoon kosher salt

3½ cups bread flour

5 tablespoons aquafaba, divided

1 tablespoon olive oil

cornmeal, for dusting

1 teaspoon granulated garlic

1. In the bowl of your stand mixer, combine the yeast, sugar, salt, and bread flour, and mix until everything is combined. Using the dough hook on medium speed, mix in 1½ cups warm (100 to 105°F) water and 3 tablespoons of the aquafaba. Continue to knead the dough on medium speed until it is smoother and elastic. The dough will be sticky but should bounce back a bit if poked.

2. Put the olive oil in a clean bowl and transfer the dough to the bowl. Toss to coat with the oil, cover, and leave in a warm area for 1 to 2 hours or until it's doubled in size.

3. Preheat your oven to 500°F. Turn a baking tray or large cast-iron skillet upside down and place in the oven to preheat on the upper middle rack.

4. Turn the dough out onto a lightly floured surface and press out the air. Knead it by hand for a few turns, then shape into a ball. If you have a pizza peel, move this ball onto your prepared peel. If not, sprinkle some cornmeal on an upside-down baking tray and place your blob of dough on this. Shape the dough ball into a pizza (or two), making sure if you're using a cast iron in your oven not to make the pizza bigger than your cast-iron skillet!.

5. Top the pizza with your sauce and toppings. Brush the remaining aquafaba onto the crust edges and sprinkle these parts with the granulated garlic. Allow the pizza to rise another 20 minutes.

6. Transfer the pizza into the oven, using your baking tray like a pizza peel. Bake for 15 to 25 minutes, depending on your oven. The bottom of the crust should be browned and the toppings should be slightly charred and/or bubbling. Serve immediately.

YIELD: 1 to 2 pizzas   PREP TIME: 30 minutes, plus rising times   COOK TIME: 15 to 25 minutes

❋ Pesto Flatbread

This garlic-laden flatbread just begs to be made in summer during the height of heirloom tomato season. Serve with sliced tomatoes, a drizzle of fruity olive oil, and high-quality balsamic vinegar.

½ cup aquafaba, divided

1 large bunch basil or 2 cups chopped leaves

3 cloves garlic, crushed

3 teaspoons coarse sea salt, divided

2¼ teaspoons instant yeast

1 tablespoon sugar

3½ cups bread flour

1 tablespoon olive oil

cornmeal, for dusting

⅓ cup pine nuts

1. To make the pesto, in a food processor, combine 3 tablespoons of the aquafaba with the basil, garlic, and 2 teaspoons of salt until everything is blitzed into a paste.

2. In the bowl of your stand mixer, combine the yeast, sugar, the remaining teaspoon salt, and bread flour, and mix until everything is combined. Using the dough hook on medium speed, mix in 1½ cups warm (100 to 105°F) water, pesto mix, and 3 tablespoons of the aquafaba. Continue to knead the dough on medium speed until it is smoother and elastic. The dough will be sticky but should bounce back a bit if poked.

3. Put the olive oil in a clean bowl and transfer the dough to the bowl. Toss to coat with the oil, cover, and leave in a warm area for 1 to 2 hours or until it's doubled in size.

4. Preheat your oven to 500°F. Turn a baking tray or large cast-iron skillet upside down, and place in the oven to preheat on the upper middle rack.

5. Turn the dough out onto a lightly floured surface and press out a lot of the air. Knead it by hand for a few turns, then shape into a ball. If you have a pizza peel, move this ball onto your prepared peel. If not, sprinkle some cornmeal on an upside-down baking tray and place your blob of dough on this. Shape the dough ball into a long rectangle (or two), making sure if you're using a cast iron in your oven not to make the flatbread bigger than your cast-iron skillet.

6. Brush the remaining aquafaba onto the flatbread and sprinkle these parts with the pine nuts. Allow the flatbread to rise another 30 minutes in a warm place.

7. Transfer the bread into the oven, using your baking tray like a pizza peel. Bake for 30 to 45 minutes, depending on your oven. If the pine nuts start to burn, cover the bread with tin foil. The bottom of the crust should be browned and the bread should sound hollow if tapped on the bottom once done. Allow to cool before cutting.

YIELD: 1 to 2 flatbreads   PREP TIME: 30 minutes, plus rising times   COOK TIME: 30 to 45 minutes

# Biscuits

Using homemade butter allows you to make vegan biscuits without shortening. The flakes are still there and the flavor is better than ever.

1 teaspoon vinegar	2 teaspoons sugar
1 cup almond milk	1 teaspoon kosher salt
2 cups all-purpose flour	¼ teaspoon ground black pepper
2 tablespoons baking powder	⅔ cup cubed Aquafaba Butter (page 128), cold

1. Mix the vinegar into the almond milk and set aside until milk is slightly thickened and tangy, about 5 minutes.

2. Prepare a baking sheet by lining it with parchment paper.

3. In a large bowl, sift together the flour, baking powder, sugar, salt, and pepper.

4. Cut in the butter using a pastry cutter/dough blender or a couple of forks, or by pulsing the mix in a food processor. Mix until the dough resembles coarse sand.

5. Add the milk to the flour mixture, and stir using a firm spoon or spatula. Stir until just combined into a rough, shaggy dough.

6. Preheat the oven to 425°F.

7. Press the dough out onto a lightly floured surface into a rectangle. Fold the rectangle over itself and gently but firmly press the dough down into another rectangle, the same size as the original. Fold the dough over once more and press down until the dough is about 1-inch tall. Cover with a kitchen towel and allow to rest for half an hour.

8. Press down on the dough one more time until your rectangle is about 9 x 7 inches. Using a biscuit cutter or a glass, cut out biscuits. You can reuse the scrap dough one more time.

9. Bake 10 to 15 minutes or until the biscuits have risen and are golden brown.

YIELD: about 20 biscuits   PREP TIME: 15 minutes, plus 30 minutes resting time   COOK TIME: 10 to 15 minutes

❋ Hearty Whole Wheat Flatbread

This hearty whole wheat flatbread goes great with the aquafaba Hummus (page 135), some olives, and fresh crudité.

2¼ teaspoons instant yeast

1 tablespoon sugar

1 teaspoon kosher salt

3½ cups whole wheat flour

6 tablespoons aquafaba, divided

1 tablespoon olive oil

cornmeal, for dusting

2 tablespoons sesame seeds

1 tablespoon flaky sea salt

1. In the bowl of your stand mixer, combine the yeast, sugar, salt, and flour, and mix until everything is combined. Using the dough hook on medium speed, mix in 1½ cups warm (100 to 105°F) water and 3 tablespoons of the aquafaba. Continue to knead the dough on medium speed until it is smoother and elastic. The dough will be sticky but should bounce back a bit if poked.

2. Put the olive oil in a clean bowl and transfer the dough to the bowl. Toss to coat with the oil, cover, and leave in a warm area for 1 to 2 hours or until it's double in size.

3. Preheat your oven to 500°F. Turn a baking tray or large cast-iron skillet upside down and place in the oven to preheat on the upper middle rack.

4. Turn the dough out onto a lightly floured surface and press out a lot of the air. Knead it by hand for a few turns, then shape it into a ball. If you have a pizza peel, move this ball onto your prepared peel. If not, sprinkle some cornmeal on an upside-down baking tray and place your blob of dough on this. Shape the dough ball into a pizza (or two), making sure if you're using a cast iron in your oven not to make the pizza bigger than your cast-iron skillet!

5. Brush the remaining aquafaba onto the flatbread and sprinkle these parts with the sesame seeds and flake salt. Allow the flatbread to rise another 30 minutes in a warm place.

6. Transfer the bread into the oven, using your baking tray like a pizza peel. Bake for 30 to 45 minutes, depending on your oven. If the sesame seeds start to burn, cover the bread with tin foil. The bottom of the crust should be browned and the bread should sound hollow if tapped on the bottom once done. Allow to cool before cutting.

YIELD: 1 to 2 flatbreads   PREP TIME: 30 minutes, plus rising times   COOK TIME: 30 to 45 minutes

❋ Cornbread Muffins

Served warm, split open, and slathered with homemade Aquafaba Butter (page 128), this dish is the perfect side to bring on a picnic or to serve with collard greens and a big ole' pot of beans. I like to drizzle mine with some agave.

3 cups all-purpose flour	1 cup sugar
2 tablespoons baking powder	1½ cups coconut milk, cream included
1½ teaspoons kosher salt	½ cup coconut oil, melted
1 cup cornmeal	¼ cup plus 2 tablespoons aquafaba
pinch cayenne pepper, optional	

1. Preheat the oven to 375°F. Prepare a muffin tin with liners.

2. In a large bowl, stir together the flour, baking powder, salt, cornmeal, cayenne, and sugar.

3. Stir the coconut milk, melted coconut oil, and aquafaba into the cornmeal mixture until just combined.

4. Scoop the muffins into the prepared muffin tin.

5. Bake for 30 to 35 minutes or until the muffins have puffed up and the tops are golden.

6. Allow to cool completely before serving.

YIELD: **12 muffins**   PREP TIME: **10 minutes**   COOK TIME: **30 to 35 minutes**

❋ Buckwheat Crepes

While traditional crepes definitely have a Parisian feel to them, I find eating buckwheat crepes feels a lot more exotic. Perhaps it's a symptom of how prevalent creperies have become in US shopping malls. Buckwheat crepes are a staple of many Eastern European cuisines but they are most famous in France. (That should be no surprise.) I like to add a hint of sugar to mine but you can omit it if you are watching sugar levels. I love to fill these with roasted portobello strips or tofu scrambles. Make this batter overnight for an elegant breakfast in no time.

¼ cup aquafaba

1 cup buckwheat flour

1 cup almond milk

½ teaspoon kosher salt

1 teaspoon sugar

1 tablespoon coconut oil, melted

¼ to ½ cup of water

1. In a small bowl, whisk your aquafaba to break it up; it should start to froth up.

2. Add the aquafaba, flour, milk, salt, and sugar to a blender. Blend on high for about 30 seconds or until no lumps appear. Let the batter rest overnight. This helps to soften the buckwheat and give it time to soak up all the liquid.

3. Right before you're ready to use the batter, add a couple of tablespoons of water to the batter and blend it again. Slowly add the coconut oil while blending. If the batter is still too thick, continue adding water, a couple tablespoons at a time, and blending until you have a pourable, thin batter. This usually takes between ¼ to ½ cup of water.

4. Set your stove to medium-high heat, and coat a large pan or skillet with nonstick cooking spray. Let the pan get nice and hot.

5. Once the pan is hot, ladle a ¼-cup scoop of batter. Immediately use an off-set spatula, the back of a spoon, or simply a rapid swirling motion of the pan to spread the batter out into an even, thin circle.

6. Let the bottom of the crepe start to get golden brown, and flip carefully. The crepe should be ready to flip after about 30 seconds. Cook for another 30 seconds or until both sides are golden.

7. Stack the crepes on top of one another as you cook the rest; this keeps them soft and warm.

8. Fill with whatever your heart desires and serve.

YIELD: about 10 crepes   PREP TIME: 10 minutes, plus overnight rest   COOK TIME: 10 minutes

✳ Savory Crepes

Like with the sweet crepes, you will need a nice nonstick pan for this recipe. And don't fret if they don't come out perfect in the first round! Everyone loses the first one or two. I like a lot of herbs in my crepes and will change them up depending on what's going inside. If I'm filling them with something like curried chickpeas, I add some toasted cumin seeds. Cumin works great in any curry dish and many Mexican-inspired ones as well.

⅔ cup aquafaba

1¼ cups whole wheat flour

½ teaspoon kosher salt

¼ to ½ cup almond milk, depending on thickness of batter

1 tablespoon coconut oil, melted

2 tablespoons chopped parsley

1 very thinly sliced green onion, green parts only, optional

1½ tablespoons toasted cumin seeds, optional

1. In a small bowl, whisk your aquafaba to break it up; it should start to froth up.

2. In a separate bowl, mix the whole wheat flour with the salt.

3. Stir in the aquafaba, ¼ cup of almond milk, coconut oil, chopped parsley, green onion, and toasted cumin seeds, if using. The batter should be pourable and smooth, about the texture of coconut milk.

4. Set your stove to medium-high heat, and coat a large pan or skillet with nonstick cooking spray. Let the pan get nice and hot.

5. Once the pan is hot, ladle a ¼-cup scoop of batter. Immediately use an off-set spatula, the back of a spoon, or simply a rapid swirling motion of the pan to spread the batter out into an even, thin circle.

6. Let the bottom of the crepe start to get golden brown, and flip carefully. The crepe should be ready to flip after about 30 seconds. Cook for another 30 seconds or until both sides are golden.

7. Stack the crepes on top of one another as you cook the rest; this keeps them soft and warm.

8. Serve as a side dish or stuffed with your favorite fillings.

YIELD: about 10 crepes   PREP TIME: 10 minutes   COOK TIME: 10 minutes

✳ Savory Scones

These scones used to be but a mere memory for many vegans. Now you can have this delightfully savory baked good and know every single ingredient that goes into them is cruelty free and all natural.

½ teaspoon vinegar

½ cup plus 2 tablespoon almond milk, divided

2¾ cups all-purpose flour

1 teaspoon kosher salt

1 tablespoon baking powder

½ teaspoon ground pepper

¼ cup plus 2 tablespoons aquafaba

½ cup cold Aquafaba Butter (page 128), cubed

1¼ cups shredded Cheddar cheese (page 124), divided

½ cup crumbled Smoky Rice Paper Bacon (page 26)

1. In a small bowl, mix the vinegar into ½ cup of the almond milk, and set aside until milk is slightly thickened and tangy, about 5 minutes.

2. Prepare a baking sheet by lining it with parchment paper.

3. In a large bowl, sift together the flour, salt, pepper, and baking powder. Add the aquafaba to the milk mixture and stir. Set aside.

4. Cut in the butter using a pastry cutter/dough blender or a couple of forks, or by pulsing the mix in a food processor. Mix until the dough is full of pebbles of butter. These "pebbles" do not need to be the same size, and some variation is preferred. This gives the scone its texture. You want this to be just undermixed.

5. Mix in the 1 cup of the cheddar and all of the bacon. Add the milk to the flour mixture and stir using a firm spoon or spatula. Stir until just combined.

6. Lightly flour the prepared baking sheet. Divide the dough into two equal pieces. Shape these pieces on the baking sheet into circles about 6 inches in diameter. Brush the tops of the circles with the 2 tablespoons of milk. Sprinkle with the remaining cheddar.

7. Run a sharp knife under cold water and cut the circles into 6 pieces each. Separate the pieces from one another until there is a space of ½ inch between them.

8. Place the scones in the freezer for 30 minutes. While the scones chill, preheat the oven to 425°F.

9. Bake the scones for about 25 minutes or until they are golden brown. Cool for 5 minutes and serve warm.

YIELD: 12 scones   PREP TIME: 5 to 10 minutes, plus 30 minutes of chilling   COOK TIME: 25 minutes

 # Dinner Rolls

Your holiday (or even regular weeknight) dinner table can now be complete with this recipe for the classic dinner roll. I call for instant dry yeast in this recipe, as it allows me to skip the proofing stage in the beginning. If you only have active dry yeast, help it to "wake up" by mixing it with ¼ cup of warm water and 1 tablespoon of maple and allowing to sit for 10 minutes or until the yeast foams.

2½ teaspoons instant dry yeast

2 cups all-purpose flour

¼ teaspoon kosher salt

¾ cup full-fat coconut milk

2 tablespoons maple syrup

2 tablespoons Aquafaba Butter (page 128)

2 tablespoons aquafaba

1. In a stand mixer with the dough hook attachment, stir together the yeast, flour, and salt on low speed.

2. In a small saucepan, mix together the milk, maple, and butter, and heat until the butter is melted and the milk is around 105 to 110°F.

3. With the mixer still running, pour in the milk mixture. Once fully combined, turn speed up to medium. Knead on medium speed for about 5 minutes or until you have a smooth dough.

5. Spray a 9-inch cake pan with nonstick spray. Divide the dough into 12 equal pieces and place in the cake pan, with some space between each. Cover loosely with oiled plastic wrap, then with a clean kitchen towel, and leave to rise somewhere warm (but not hot!) for about 40 minutes or until your dough has doubled in size. If using active dry yeast, this may take up to 60 minutes. Go by the size of the dough, not the time passed.

6. Preheat your oven to 425°F while the rolls rise. Position a rack in the middle of the oven. 20 minutes before baking the loaves, put a glass or metal baking dish filled with 3 to 4 cups of water (depending on the size of your pan) on the bottom of the oven. This creates steam that will make a better crust.

7. Once ready to bake, remove the plastic wrap. Brush the rolls with the aquafaba. Place pan in the oven and immediately lower the temperature to 350°F.

8. After 10 minutes of baking, remove the water and continue baking for another 20 to 30 minutes, or until the rolls have grown in size and the tops are golden. Let cool for 10 minutes before serving.

YIELD: 12 rolls   PREP TIME: 10 minutes, plus rising times   COOK TIME: 30 to 40 minutes

🌸 Mushroom Pot Pie

Mushrooms are so fantastically firm, rich, and full of umami flavor. This recipe is perfect if you've got a hungry crowd to feed. It's great for dinner, lunch, or a late-night-raid-the-fridge kind of snack.

1 ounce dried porcini mushrooms, chopped into bits

2 tablespoons olive oil

1 pound wild mushrooms

1 medium onion, diced

2 celery stalks, diced

2 carrots, diced

2 cups diced russet potatoes (about one small potato)

1 tablespoon thyme leaves

2 tablespoons chopped parsley

2 bay leaves

¼ cup flour

1 cup vegetable broth

salt and pepper, to taste

1 recipe Quiche Crust (page 27)

3 tablespoons aquafaba, for brushing

1. Rehydrate the porcinis in 1 cup of boiling water. Set aside for at least 10 minutes while you prepare the remaining ingredients.

2. In a large dutch oven or heavy bottomed pot over medium-high heat, warm up the olive oil until it is shimmering. Add the mushrooms, onion, celery, carrots, and potatoes. Cook, stirring occasionally, until the veggies are softer but not mushy, about 5 to 7 minutes. Add the herbs.

3. Sprinkle the flour over the top of the mixture and stir to coat, still on the heat. Any moisture from the vegetables should start to get absorbed by the flour. Slowly add the vegetable broth, soaked porcinis, and their soaking water, stirring to incorporate everything and prevent the flour from clumping. Add salt and pepper to taste. Set aside and allow to cool completely.

4. Line a 9-inch pie pan or an 8 x 8-inch casserole dish with the prepared Quiche Crust dough. (Dough should be rolled out to ⅛-inch thick.) Add cooled veggie filling to the pie, pressing down if needed, to fit everything in. Top with more pie dough. Crimp edges and make some slices in the top to create vents for steam. Chill for 30 minutes in the fridge.

5. Preheat your oven to 425°F. Brush the tops of the pie dough with the aquafaba and bake in the lower middle section of the oven for 35 to 40 minutes or until the top is golden and the mixture inside can be seen trying to bubble out of the steam vents.

6. Allow to cool for 5 minutes and serve.

YIELD: 1 large (9-inch-wide circle or 8 x 8-inch square) pot pie   PREP TIME: 20 minutes, plus 30 minutes cooling time   COOK TIME: 35 to 40 minutes

 # Mozzarella Cheese

Use this easy-to-make mozzarella on your homemade pizza. If you only want this cheese to melt (and say, stay gooey on a pizza), you can omit the carrageenan. The carrageenan is essential, however, to making a cheese that is sliceable. If you want to turn this into mozzarella sticks, you'll want to allow the cheese to set in a rectangular mold, like a loaf pan.

½ cup cashews, soaked for at least 4 hours

1 cup aquafaba

2 tablespoons corn or tapioca flour/starch

1 tablespoon carrageenan

1 teaspoon lemon juice

1 tablespoon nutritional yeast

1 teaspoon white miso paste

½ teaspoon sea salt

¼ cup plus 1 tablespoon coconut oil

1. In a high-speed blender, blend the drained cashews with the aquafaba until it is as smooth as possible. If you find your mixture is lumpy, do not add water! Instead, strain your mixture by gently pressing it through a fine-mesh sieve.

2. Return this mixture to the blender and add the tapioca starch, carrageenan, lemon juice, nutritional yeast, miso, and salt, and mix until thoroughly combined.

3. Slowly drizzle in the coconut oil while blending. The mixture should be thick but blendable and completely smooth.

4. Transfer the cheese mix to a medium-size pot and cook on medium-low heat while stirring constantly. As the tapioca starch begins to activate, the cheese will start to form some lumps. The mix will begin to resemble classically melted cheese as it heats up. You'll start to see bubbling on the sides of the pot, and the cheese should look glossy and smooth. When it reaches 170°F, it is ready for the next step. Alternatively, if you have a high-speed blender like a Vitamix, you can make this entire recipe in the blender, allowing it to run on high speed until you hit 170°F. Once you have reached 170°F, remove the cheese from the heat.

5. Pour the cheese mixture into a small, lightly greased glass bowl. Refrigerate for a few hours to fully firm up the cheese before slicing or grating. The cheese will continue to thicken as it firms up.

YIELD: **1** block   PREP TIME: **5** minutes   COOK TIME: **10** minutes, plus overnight rest

❋ Baked Mozzarella Sticks

For this recipe, you will need to cut your mozzarella into sticks resembling the string cheese sold in grocery stores. This task is made a lot easier if you make your cheese in a loaf pan, or otherwise rectangular/square pan, as opposed to a round pan.

¼ cup whole wheat panko bread crumbs

¼ cup regular bread crumbs

1 teaspoon dried oregano

1 teaspoon kosher salt, or more to taste

black pepper, to taste

2 tablespoons aquafaba

¼ cup flour

1 batch Mozzarella Cheese (page 122), cut into 20 strips and frozen

1. In a large bowl, mix together the panko bread crumbs, regular bread crumbs, dried oregano, salt, and pepper. Set aside

2. In a small bowl, whisk the aquafaba until it is just frothy and loosened.

3. Pour the flour onto a plate.

4. Dip a frozen mozzarella stick into the aquafaba and then roll in the flour. Dip it back into the aquafaba and then into the bread crumb mix. Set aside and repeat with the remaining mozzarella strips. Freeze the strips for at least an hour. This is crucial, as it prevents the cheese from melting out before done.

5. While the sticks are freezing, preheat your oven to 425°F. Position an oven rack in the lower middle half.

6. Once the sticks are ready for cooking, prepare a baking tray by lining it with tin foil and spraying it with nonstick cooking spray or wiping it lightly with oil.

7. Bake the sticks for 5 minutes, flip, and bake another 5 minutes, or until the crumbs are golden brown.

8. Serve warm.

YIELD: 20   PREP TIME: 10 minutes, plus 1 hour freezing time   COOK TIME: 10 minutes

❀ Cheddar Cheese

Finally, a meltable vegan cheese that you can make at home! Use this in/on cheddar biscuits. This recipe was inspired greatly by the blog Avocados and Ales. You can use this base cheese recipe, as I have, as a starting point for making all of the great springy and meltable cheeses that have been missing from the vegan scene for too long! If you only want this cheese to melt (and say, stay gooey on a pizza) you can omit the carrageenan. The carrageenan is essential, however, to making a cheese that is sliceable.

½ cup raw sunflower seeds, soaked for at least 2 hours

1 cup aquafaba

½ of a roasted red pepper (canned in fine)

2 tablespoons corn or tapioca flour/starch

4 teaspoons carrageenan

½ teaspoon lemon juice

1 tablespoon nutritional yeast

2 teaspoons red miso paste

¼ teaspoon paprika

¾ teaspoon kosher salt

¼ cup plus 2 tablespoons refined coconut oil, liquid

1 teaspoon apple cider vinegar

1. In a high-speed blender, blend the drained sunflower seeds with the aquafaba and roasted red pepper until as smooth as possible. If you find your mixture is lumpy, do not add water! Instead, strain your mixture by gently pressing it through a fine-mesh sieve.

2. Return this mixture to the blender and add the tapioca starch, carrageenan, lemon juice, nutritional yeast, miso, paprika, and salt, and mix until thoroughly combined.

3. Slowly drizzle in the coconut oil while blending. The mixture should be thick but blendable and completely smooth.

4. Transfer the cheese mix to a medium-size pot, and cook on medium-low heat while stirring constantly. As the tapioca starch begins to activate, the cheese will start to form some lumps. The mix will begin to resemble classically melted cheese as it heats up. You'll start to see bubbling on the sides of the pot and the cheese should look glossy and smooth. When it reaches 170°F, it is ready for the next step. Alternatively, if you have a high-speed blender like a Vitamix, you can make this entire recipe in the blender, allowing it to run on high speed until you hit 170°F.

5. Once you have reached 170°F, add the apple cider vinegar, blend until combined, and remove the cheese from the heat.

6. Pour the cheese mixture into a small, lightly greased glass bowl. Refrigerate for a few hours to fully firm up the cheese before slicing or grating. The cheese will continue to thicken as it firms up.

YIELD: **1 block**   PREP TIME: **5 minutes**   COOK TIME: **10 minutes**, plus a few hours refrigeration

✳ AF Cream Cheese

Tangy, delicious, spreadable cream cheese. Perfect for morning sandwiches or homemade cheesecakes! Whip it up the night before for a wonderfully fulfilling morning meal.

1 cup cashews, soaked for at least 4 hours	¼ teaspoon kosher salt
1 tablespoon lemon juice	⅓ cup refined coconut oil, liquid
¼ cup aquafaba	1 tablespoon olive oil

1. Using a high-speed blender or a food processor, blend the cashews with the lemon juice until they are as smooth as possible. Once the cashews are completely smooth, blend in the ½ cup of water. Now the mixture should be totally smooth and loosened.

2. Using a tall container and an immersion blender, blend the aquafaba and salt until it becomes light and frothy. While continuing to blend, very slowly drizzle in the coconut oil and, eventually, the olive oil. This mixture should be white and creamy and emulsified, as if you were making mayonnaise.

3. Add in the cashew cream, 1 large tablespoon at a time, blending fully between each addition. Once all of the cashew mixture has been added, transfer the cream cheese to a bowl and refrigerate overnight.

YIELD: **2 cups**   PREP TIME: **5 minutes**   COOK TIME: **15 minutes**, plus overnight refrigeration

Pepper Jack Cheese

Spicy pepper jack melts wonderfully on top of Pesto Flatbread (page 113.) If you only want this cheese to melt (and say, stay gooey on a pizza), you can omit the carrageenan. The carrageenan is essential, however, to making a cheese that is sliceable.

¼ cup cashews, soaked for at least 4 hours

¼ cup raw sunflower seeds, soaked for at least 2 hours

1 cup aquafaba

2 tablespoons corn or tapioca flour/starch

1 tablespoon carrageenan

1 teaspoon lemon juice

1 tablespoon nutritional yeast

1 teaspoon red miso paste

½ teaspoon sea salt

1½ teaspoons onion powder

1 teaspoon garlic powder

¼ cup plus 1 tablespoon coconut oil

½ cup diced pickled jalapeños

½ cup diced red bell pepper

1. In a high-speed blender, blend the drained cashews and sunflower seeds with the aquafaba until as smooth as possible. If you find your mixture is lumpy, do not add water! Instead strain your mixture by gently pressing it through a fine-mesh sieve.

2. Return this mixture to the blender and add the tapioca starch, carrageenan, lemon juice, nutritional yeast, miso, salt, onion, and garlic powder, and mix until thoroughly combined.

3. Slowly drizzle in the coconut oil while blending. The mixture should be thick but blendable and completely smooth.

4. Transfer the cheese mix to a medium-size pot, and cook on medium-low heat while stirring constantly. As the tapioca starch begins to activate, the cheese will start to form some lumps. The mix will begin to resemble classically melted cheese as it heats up. You'll start to see bubbling on the sides of the pot, and the cheese should look glossy and smooth. When it reaches 170°F, it is ready for the next step. Alternatively, if you have a high-speed blender like a Vitamix, you can make this entire recipe in the blender, allowing it to run on high speed until you hit 170°F.

5. Once you have reached 170°F, add the diced pickled jalapeños and bell peppers, and stir until combined. Remove the cheese from the heat.

6. Pour the cheese mixture into a small, lightly greased glass bowl. Refrigerate for a few hours to fully firm up the cheese before slicing or grating. The cheese will continue to thicken as it firms up.

YIELD: **1 block**   PREP TIME: **10 minutes**   COOK TIME: **10 minutes**, plus a few hours refrigeration

SPREADS AND DIPS

While these recipes may seem out of place in a baking book, the spreads and dips contained within go perfectly with many of the recipes found in the Savory Treats chapter (page 111). And besides, I couldn't pass up on showing off all of the magic tricks that aquafaba has up its sleeve. This is where you'll find out how to make your own butter (that you can use in any of the recipes in this book that call for butter), along with vegan mayo (much cheaper than store bought), the smoothest hummus (to use up some of your leftover chickpeas), and more.

 # Aquafaba Butter

Use this butter to spread on breads or to make your aquafaba buttercream (along with many other recipes in this book). I prefer to use odorless coconut oil unless I am making a coconut-flavored buttercream. Also, generally when making butter, I tend to leave the salt out and add a sprinkling of my favorite sea salt on top. This allows the butter to be used in baking, for cooking up some pancakes, or making a frosting without having to make a second unsalted batch. Remember, it's always easier to add than to take away. As with many of these recipes, this is a basic emulsion. In order to make the emulsion work properly, you're going to have to pay attention to the temperature of your aquafaba. If your kitchen is very hot then you want to use the aquafaba straight from the refrigerator. If your kitchen is cool then you can just refrigerate your aquafaba for 10 minutes to make it slightly cooler than room temperature. This butter is a variation of Nina's famous butter recipe from the Internet, found on plantepusherne.dk.

⅓ cup plus 1 tablespoon odorless coconut oil, liquid and at cool room temperature

1 tablespoon plus 1 teaspoon canola oil

3 tablespoons aquafaba, chilled

1. Stir together the two oils until well combined.

2. Using either a quart-size Mason jar or tall narrow glass container with an immersion blender, or high-speed blender, blend up the aquafaba on medium speed.

3. Turn up the speed of the blender to high if using the immersion blender, medium high if using a high-speed blender, and SLOWLY drizzle in the oil blend. A steady trickle is fine, but by no means do you want to just pour all the oil in or the emulsion will not work. This should take about 2 minutes.

4. Once your butter is the consistency of mayonnaise, it is ready to rest in the fridge. You want to give this a full overnight rest, uncovered, to set. Covering it can deflate some of the emulsion.

5. Once the butter is set, you can cover it to prevent odd fridge flavors from infiltrating it. Enjoy however you would use butter.

YIELD: ½ cup   PREP TIME: minimal   COOK TIME: 3 minutes, plus overnight refrigeration

❋ French-Style Aquafaba Butter

This tangy butter has greater depth and more robust flavor than the Aquafaba Butter recipe on the previous page. You're going to want to eat this slathered on some crusty homemade bread, crackers, or just some small radishes, with extra salt, please. The process for this is essentially the same as the previous butter, but with additions. In order to make the emulsion work properly, you're going to have to pay attention to the temperature of your aquafaba. If your kitchen is very hot then you want to use the aquafaba straight from the refrigerator. If your kitchen is cool, then you can just refrigerate your aquafaba for 10 minutes to make it slightly cooler than room temperature.

⅓ cup plus 1 tablespoon odorless coconut oil, liquid and at cool room temperature

1 tablespoon plus 1 teaspoon virgin olive oil

3 tablespoons aquafaba, chilled

½ teaspoon apple cider vinegar

⅛ teaspoon sea salt, plus more for sprinkling (fleur de sel is especially nice)

1. Stir together the two oils until well combined.

2. Using either a quart-sized Mason jar or tall narrow glass container with an immersion blender, or high-speed blender, blend the aquafaba with the apple cider vinegar and sea salt on medium speed.

3. Turn up the speed of the blender to high if using the immersion blender, medium high if using a high-speed blender, and SLOWLY drizzle in the oil blend. A steady trickle is fine; by no means do you want to just pour all the oil in or the emulsion will not work. This should take about 2 minutes.

4. Once your butter is the consistency of mayonnaise, it is ready to rest in the fridge. You want to give this a full overnight rest, uncovered to set. Covering it can deflate some of the emulsion.

5. Once the butter is set, you can cover it to prevent odd fridge flavors from infiltrating it. Enjoy however you would use butter.

YIELD: ½ cup   PREP TIME: minimal   COOK TIME: 3 minutes, plus overnight refrigeration

 Flavored Butter

Flavored, or compound, butter, is one of the single easiest ways to impress unexpected guests. While you could make these ahead and freeze them, I find that fats love to absorb all of the funky smells that are floating around in the freezer, not to mention the dreaded freezer burn. Since this takes next to no time to whip up, I recommend making them fresh.

Pesto Butter

This flavor goes great on roasted portobello sandwiches, homemade pasta, or anything that could use a bright green Italian-esque flair. Feel free to swap out the pesto for fresh chopped herbs.

½ cup Aquafaba Butter (page 128)

2 tablespoons vegan pesto

1 tablespoon chopped pistachios

1. Using a firm spatula, beat the butter in a shallow bowl until soft and whipped.

2. Stir in the pesto and whip until almost fully combined. Fold in the chopped pistachios. Refrigerate for at least 30 minutes to an hour to help the butter set before using.

YIELD: ½ to ⅔ cup   PREP TIME: 10 minutes, plus 30 minutes to 1 hour refrigeration   COOK TIME: none

Hazelnut Butter

This is my go-to butter for sourdough toast and buckwheat AF pancakes (drizzled with maple for extra indulgence.) Peanuts give a nice Southern vibe to this recipe when used in place of the hazelnuts.

2 tablespoons toasted hazelnuts

½ cup French-Style Aquafaba Butter (page 129)

1. Grind the hazelnuts in either a mortar and pestle or a food processor.

2. Using a firm spatula, beat the butter in a shallow bowl until soft and whipped.

3. Fold in the ground hazelnuts. Refrigerate for at least 30 minutes to an hour to help the butter set before using.

YIELD: ½ to ⅔ cup   PREP TIME: minimal   COOK TIME: 10 minutes, plus 30 minutes to 1 hour refrigeration

Aquafaba Mayonnaise

Mayonnaise is an emulsion that historically has benefitted from the naturally occurring lecithin found in egg yolks. Having a high-powered blender or a stick blender will help whip up classically tasting mayonnaise in less than 3 minutes' time. This recipe uses a tip from The Food Lab's J. Kenji Lopez-Alt and adds whole chickpeas to replace the lecithin, though you could use soy granules if you have them on hand. Once you've mastered mayonnaise you're ready to tackle the next line of sauces, aioli, and hollandaise.

3 tablespoons aquafaba

1 tablespoon apple cider vinegar

½ teaspoon ground mustard

12 cooked chickpeas or ⅛ teaspoon soy lecithin granules

½ teaspoon sea salt, plus more to taste, if desired

½ cup avocado or vegetable oil

¼ cup extra-virgin olive oil

black pepper, to taste

kosher salt, to taste

1. Using either a wide-mouth quart jar (or other vessel that can fit your immersion blender) or the carafe of your high-speed blender, combine the aquafaba, cider vinegar, ground mustard, chickpeas, and salt. Run the blender on high and combine everything until it is smooth.

2. With the blender still running, slowly drizzle in the avocado oil, working ¼ cup at a time, taking care to not pour in too much oil at once. Do not start on the next ¼ cup until the first is totally and completely whipped into the chickpea mixture.

3. Repeat step 2 with the extra-virgin olive oil, but stop the blending once this oil is completely mixed in and the mixture resembles mayonnaise. The flavors of the extra-virgin olive oil are prone to oxidization when blended at such a high speed. I personally do not find it to be a big enough difference to require hand-whisking this in, but you can if you notice the difference. Taste and add pepper and salt, to taste, by hand.

4. Store in the fridge for up to a week.

YIELD: **1 cup**   PREP TIME: **3 minutes**   COOK TIME: **none**

 # Aioli

Aioli is a sauce that is prepared in a similar manner as mayonnaise. It's so similar, in fact, that I often make an "aioli hack" by starting with a base of already-made mayonnaise.

2 cloves garlic

½ teaspoon kosher salt

1 cup Aquafaba Mayonnaise (page 131)

2 tablespoons extra-virgin olive oil

2 tablespoons finely chopped herbs (I prefer oregano to pair with Mediterranean meals, cilantro for Mexican, basil for Italian, etc.), optional

1. Using either a mortar and pestle or a small dish and the back of a fork, mash the garlic with the salt until a wet paste forms.

2. Whisk the paste into the mayonnaise, and then whisk in the olive oil. I usually do this with the fork I mashed the garlic with.

3. Stir in the herbs, if using.

YIELD: **1 cup**   PREP TIME: **3 minutes**   COOK TIME: **none**

✿ Hollandaise

Hollandaise is the fanciest way to dress up your brunch. Nothing says classy like steamed asparagus topped with this French "Mother Sauce." If you have any black salt (kala namak), a pinch will work wonders in this recipe to recreate the "eggy" flavor.

¼ cup aquafaba

1 teaspoon smooth Dijon mustard

3 tablespoons lemon juice

½ teaspoon sea salt, plus more to taste if desired

pinch black salt

2 tablespoons Aquafaba Butter (page 128), melted

2 tablespoons extra-virgin olive oil

pepper, to taste

kosher salt, to taste

1. Using either a wide-mouth quart jar (or other vessel that can fit your immersion blender) or the carafe of your high-speed blender, combine the AF, mustard, lemon juice, and salts. Run the blender on high, and combine everything until it is smooth.

2. With the blender still running, slowly drizzle in the melted butter, taking care to not pour in too much at once. Do not start on the oil until the butter is totally and completely whipped into the mixture.

3. Repeat step 2 with the extra-virgin olive oil, but stop the blending once this oil is completely mixed in and the mixture is thick and creamy but pourable. The flavors of the extra-virgin olive oil are prone to oxidization when blended at such a high speed. I personally do not find it to be a big enough difference to require hand-whisking this in, but you can if you notice the difference. Taste and add pepper and salt, to taste, by hand.

4. Store in the fridge for up to a week.

YIELD: **1 cup**   PREP TIME: **3 minutes**   COOK TIME: none

# Queso Dip

Use your homemade cheeses to assemble this delightful dip that's perfect for entertaining.

1 cup Pepper Jack Cheese (page 126), cubed

1 cup Cheddar Cheese (page 124), cubed

¾ cup salsa, as spicy as you like

1 garlic clove, minced

1 green onion, sliced

pickled jalapeño slices, for topping, optional

tortilla chips or hearty crackers, to serve

1. In a medium pot on medium-low heat, stir together all of the ingredients except for the pickled jalapeño slices and crackers. Cook, stirring frequently, until everything is melted.

2. Transfer to a small bowl or casserole dish and serve, topped with the pickled jalapeño slices and chips/crackers.

YIELD: **about 3 cups**   PREP TIME: **5 to 10 minutes**   COOK TIME: **10 minutes**

 # Hummus

A snacking classic in any kitchen, hummus is often surprisingly heavy due to all of the oil needed to make the spread smooth. Aquafaba serves as a surprising secret ingredient that allows you to cut the oil and make your own hummus in less time than it takes to run to the store!

1 (15-ounce) can chickpeas, drained and aquafaba reserved, or 2 cups cooked chickpeas and ⅔ cup aquafaba

2 cloves garlic

3 tablespoons lemon juice

¼ cup tahini

1 tablespoon olive oil

salt and black pepper, to taste

1. Using a food processor, combine the chickpeas, garlic cloves, lemon juice, tahini, and olive oil until it forms a thick paste. Make sure to scrape the sides of your food processor with a spatula so that everything is mixed.

2. While the food processor is running, slowly drizzle in the reserved aquafaba, using anywhere from ¼ to ½ cup until the hummus is smooth and creamy. More aquafaba will make a lighter hummus. Add salt and pepper to taste.

YIELD: about 3 cups   PREP TIME: minimal   COOK TIME: 10 minutes

CONVERSIONS

VOLUME CONVERSIONS

U.S.	U.S. EQUIVALENT	METRIC
1 tablespoon (3 teaspoons)	½ fluid ounce	15 milliliters
¼ cup	2 fluid ounces	60 milliliters
⅓ cup	3 fluid ounces	90 milliliters
½ cup	4 fluid ounces	120 milliliters
⅔ cup	5 fluid ounces	150 milliliters
¾ cup	6 fluid ounces	180 milliliters
1 cup	8 fluid ounces	240 milliliters
2 cups	16 fluid ounces	480 milliliters

WEIGHT CONVERSIONS

U.S.	METRIC
½ ounce	15 grams
1 ounce	30 grams
2 ounces	60 grams
¼ pound	115 grams
⅓ pound	150 grams
½ pound	225 grams
¾ pound	350 grams
1 pound	450 grams